Taste of Home

Summer Potlucks

TASTE OF HOME BOOKS • RDA ENTHUSIAST BRANDS, LLC • MILWAUKEE, WI

Visit us at **tasteofhome.com** for other Taste of Home books and products.

ISBN: 979-8-88977-176-0

Content Directors:
Ellie Martin Cliffe, Mark Hagen
Creative Director:
Raeann Thompson
Associate Creative Director:
Jami Geittmann
Senior Editor:
Christine Rukavena
Senior Art Director:
Courtney Lovetere
Manager, Production Design:
Satyandra Raghav
Assistant Art Director:
Jogesh Antony
Print Production Artist:
Akash Christopher
Deputy Editor, Copy Desk:
Ann M. Walter
Contributing Copy Editor:
Pam Grandy

Cover Photography
Photographer:
Dan Roberts
Set Stylist:
Melissa Franco
Food Stylists:
Joshua Rink, Ellen Crowley

Pictured on front cover:
Glazed Spatchcocked Chicken, p. 83; Strawberry Kale Salad, p. 23; Mexican Street Corn, p. 87; Smoked Pork Butt, p. 74

Pictured on back cover:
Layered Salad for a Crowd, p. 20; Jimmy's Bang Bang Chicken Sliders, p. 64; Berry Dream Cake, p. 105

Printed in China
1 3 5 7 9 10 8 6 4 2

Contents

p. 17

Snacks, Appetizers & More

LEMONY FRUIT COOLER

Be the life of the party with this refreshing change-of-pace beverage contribution.
—Dawn Shackelford, Fort Worth, TX

TAKES: 10 MIN.
MAKES: 10 SERVINGS (2½ QT.)

- ½ cup sugar
- ½ cup lemon juice
- 4 cups cold white grape juice
- 1 liter club soda, chilled
- 1 medium orange, halved and sliced
- ½ cup sliced strawberries
- ½ cup sliced fresh peaches
- Ice cubes, optional

1. In a punch bowl or pitcher, mix sugar and lemon juice until sugar is dissolved. Stir in grape juice.
2. To serve, stir in club soda and fruit. If desired, serve with ice.

1 CUP 107 cal., 0 fat (0 sat. fat), 0 chol., 29mg sod., 28g carb. (25g sugars, 0 fiber), 0 pro.

BOURBON CANDIED BACON DEVILED EGGS

At our house, it doesn't get any better than deviled eggs with bacon—bourbon candied bacon, that is. See if you can resist them. We can't.
—Colleen Delawder, Herndon, VA

PREP: 20 MIN. • **BAKE:** 25 MIN. + COOLING • **MAKES:** 2 DOZEN

- 2 Tbsp. brown sugar
- ¾ tsp. Dijon mustard
- ½ tsp. maple syrup
- ⅛ tsp. salt
- 2 tsp. bourbon, optional
- 4 thick-sliced bacon strips

EGGS

- 12 hard-boiled large eggs
- ¾ cup mayonnaise
- 1 Tbsp. maple syrup
- 1 Tbsp. Dijon mustard
- ¼ tsp. pepper
- ¼ tsp. ground chipotle pepper
- Minced fresh chives

1. Preheat oven to 350°. For bacon, in a small bowl, mix the brown sugar, mustard, syrup and salt. If desired, stir in bourbon. Coat bacon with brown sugar mixture. Place on a rack in a foil-lined 15x10x1-in. baking pan. Bake 25-30 minutes or until crisp. Cool completely.
2. Cut eggs in half lengthwise. Remove yolks, reserving whites. In a small bowl, mash yolks. Add mayonnaise, syrup, mustard and both types of pepper; stir until smooth. Chop bacon finely; fold half into egg yolk mixture. Spoon or pipe into egg whites. Sprinkle with the remaining bacon and the chives. Refrigerate, covered, until serving.

1 STUFFED EGG HALF 107 cal., 9g fat (2g sat. fat), 97mg chol., 142mg sod., 2g carb. (2g sugars, 0 fiber), 4g pro.

SLOW-COOKER MEATBALLS

You'll usually find a batch of these meatballs in my freezer. The slightly sweet sauce nicely complements the spicy pork sausage.
—Genie Brown, Roanoke, VA

PREP: 25 MIN. • **BAKE:** 15 MIN. • **MAKES:** ABOUT 4 DOZEN

- 2 lbs. bulk spicy pork sausage
- 1 large egg, lightly beaten
- 1 cup packed brown sugar
- 1 cup red wine vinegar
- 1 cup ketchup
- 1 Tbsp. soy sauce
- 1 tsp. ground ginger

1. In a large bowl, combine the sausage and egg. Shape into 1-in. balls. Place on a greased rack in a shallow baking pan. Bake at 400° for 15-20 minutes or until a thermometer reads 160°; drain.
2. Meanwhile, in a small saucepan, combine the remaining ingredients. Bring to a boil. Reduce heat; simmer, uncovered, until sugar is dissolved.
3. Transfer meatballs to a 3-qt. slow cooker. Add the sauce and stir gently to coat. Cover and keep warm on low until serving.

1 MEATBALL 70 cal., 4g fat (1g sat. fat), 14mg chol., 200mg sod., 6g carb. (6g sugars, 0 fiber), 2g pro.

MARYLAND CORN POPS

Fresh-picked sweet corn is a big thing in Maryland. Here's my homespun version of Mexican street corn that brings in local bay flavors.
—Kristie Schley, Pasadena, MD

PREP: 25 MIN. • **GRILL:** 10 MIN.
MAKES: 2 DOZEN

- 8 medium ears sweet corn, husked
- 2 Tbsp. canola oil
- 1½ cups mayonnaise
- 1½ tsp. garlic powder
- ¼ tsp. freshly ground pepper
- 24 corncob holders
- 2 cups crumbled feta cheese
- 2 Tbsp. seafood seasoning
- ¼ cup minced fresh cilantro
- Lime wedges, optional

1. Brush all sides of corn with oil. Grill, covered, over medium heat until tender and lightly browned, 10-12 minutes, turning occasionally. Remove from grill; cool slightly.
2. Meanwhile, in a small bowl, mix mayonnaise, garlic powder and pepper. Cut each ear of corn into thirds. Insert 1 corncob holder into each piece. Spread corn with mayonnaise mixture; sprinkle with cheese, seafood seasoning and cilantro. If desired, serve with lime wedges.

1 CORN POP 164 cal., 14g fat (3g sat. fat), 10mg chol., 336mg sod., 7g carb. (2g sugars, 1g fiber), 3g pro.

HAM & CHEESE PUFFS

These marvelous little bites go over well with kids of all ages. They're also good with soups and many of the items you'd expect to find on a buffet table.
—Marvin Buffington, Burlington, IA

TAKES: 30 MIN. • **MAKES:** 2 DOZEN

- 1 pkg. (2½ oz.) thinly sliced deli ham, chopped
- 1 small onion, chopped
- ½ cup shredded Swiss cheese
- 1 large egg
- 1½ tsp. Dijon mustard
- ⅛ tsp. pepper
- 1 tube (8 oz.) refrigerated crescent rolls

1. Preheat oven to 375°. Combine the first 6 ingredients. Divide the crescent dough into 24 portions. Press into greased mini muffin cups.
2. Spoon 1 Tbsp. ham mixture into each cup. Bake until golden brown, 13-15 minutes.

1 APPETIZER 110 cal., 6g fat (2g sat. fat), 25mg chol., 263mg sod., 8g carb. (2g sugars, 0 fiber), 4g pro.

QUICK & EASY

PEACH CHAMPAGNE

I searched high and low for the perfect punch recipe and finally decided to create my own. This sipper is a big hit at parties, especially weddings. In summer I freeze fresh peaches and fresh strawberries; if you don't have fresh fruit, store-bought frozen fruit works just as well.
—Linda Hall, Evington, VA

TAKES: 10 MIN. • **MAKES:** 20 SERVINGS (3¾ QT.)

- 1 pkg. (16 oz.) frozen unsweetened sliced peaches
- 1 pkg. (14 oz.) frozen unsweetened sliced strawberries
- 2 cans (5½ oz. each) peach nectar, chilled
- 1 cup peach schnapps liqueur
- 2 liters lemon-lime soda, chilled
- 2 bottles (750 ml each) champagne or other sparkling wine, chilled

In a punch bowl, combine peaches, strawberries, nectar and liqueur. Stir in soda and champagne just before serving.

¾ CUP 135 cal., 0 fat (0 sat. fat), 0 chol., 11mg sod., 18g carb. (15g sugars, 1g fiber), 0 pro.

BUFFALO RANCH POPCORN

This zippy blend is sure to spice up your favorite snack. It's perfect for game days or movie time, or as a special after-school snack.
—Joyce McCarthy, Sussex, WI

TAKES: 10 MIN. • **MAKES:** 4 QT.

- 16 cups popped popcorn
- 3 Tbsp. Buffalo wing sauce
- 2 Tbsp. butter, melted
- ⅛ tsp. cayenne pepper
- 1 Tbsp. ranch salad dressing mix
- Additional cayenne pepper

Place popcorn in a large bowl. In a small bowl, combine the Buffalo wing sauce, butter and cayenne; drizzle over popcorn, 1 Tbsp. at a time, and toss to coat. Sprinkle with dressing mix and additional cayenne to taste; toss to coat. Serve immediately.

1 CUP 82 cal., 6g fat (2g sat. fat), 4mg chol., 395mg sod., 6g carb. (0 sugars, 1g fiber), 1g pro.

BBQ CHICKEN BITES

Chicken bites wrapped in bacon get a kick from Montreal seasoning and sweetness from barbecue sauce. We love the mix of textures.
—Kathryn Dampier, Quail Valley, CA

TAKES: 25 MIN. • **MAKES:** 1½ DOZEN

- 6 bacon strips
- ¾ lb. boneless skinless chicken breasts, cut into 1-in. cubes (about 18)
- 3 tsp. Montreal steak seasoning
- 1 tsp. prepared horseradish, optional
- ½ cup barbecue sauce

1. Preheat oven to 400°. Cut bacon crosswise into thirds. Place bacon on a microwave-safe plate lined with paper towels. Cover with additional paper towels; microwave on high 3-4 minutes or until bacon is partially cooked but not crisp.
2. Place chicken in a small bowl; sprinkle with steak seasoning and toss to coat. Wrap a bacon piece around each chicken cube; secure with a toothpick. Place cubes on a parchment-lined baking sheet.
3. Bake 10 minutes. If desired, add horseradish to barbecue sauce; brush over wrapped chicken. Bake until chicken is no longer pink and bacon is crisp, 5-10 minutes longer.

1 APPETIZER 47 cal., 2g fat (0 sat. fat), 13mg chol., 249mg sod., 3g carb. (3g sugars, 0 fiber), 5g pro.

CRAB & ARTICHOKE SLOW-COOKED DIP

Whenever my girlfriends and I get together, someone brings this rich and creamy dip and someone else brings our favorite bottle of wine. Because the recipe relies on slow-cooker convenience, it's a smart choice for busy people.
—Connie McKinney, Marshall, MO

PREP: 20 MIN. • **COOK:** 2 HOURS • **MAKES:** 3½ CUPS

- 3 cups fresh baby spinach
- 1 can (14 oz.) water-packed artichoke hearts, rinsed, drained and chopped
- 1 pkg. (8 oz.) cream cheese, softened
- 2 cups shredded Havarti cheese
- 1 can (6 oz.) lump crabmeat, drained
- ½ cup sour cream
- ⅛ tsp. salt
- ⅛ tsp. pepper
- Assorted crackers

1. In a large saucepan, bring ½ in. of water to a boil. Add the spinach; cover and boil for 3-5 minutes or until wilted. Drain.
2. In a 1½-qt. slow cooker, combine artichokes, cheeses, crabmeat, sour cream, salt, pepper and spinach. Cover and cook on low for 2-3 hours or until cheeses are melted. Serve with crackers.

¼ CUP 158 cal., 12g fat (8g sat. fat), 50mg chol., 279mg sod., 3g carb. (1g sugars, 0 fiber), 9g pro.

MAKE BABY SPINACH A STAPLE

Baby spinach is actually a variety of spinach with small flat leaves. Its tender texture makes it perfect for this warm dip. It's sold in bulk or in cellophane bags in a variety of sizes. It's already cleaned and ready to eat raw or cooked.

CRISPY SRIRACHA SPRING ROLLS

While in the Bahamas, friends suggested a restaurant that served amazing chicken spring rolls. When I got home, I created my own version. Such a great appetizer to have waiting in the freezer!
—Carla Mendres, Winnipeg, MB

PREP: 50 MIN. • **COOK:** 10 MIN./BATCH • **MAKES:** ABOUT 2 DOZEN

- 3 cups coleslaw mix (about 7 oz.)
- 3 green onions, chopped
- 1 Tbsp. soy sauce
- 1 tsp. sesame oil
- 1 lb. boneless skinless chicken breasts
- 1 tsp. seasoned salt
- 2 pkg. (8 oz. each) cream cheese, softened
- 2 Tbsp. Sriracha chili sauce
- 1 pkg. (24 to 28 each) spring roll wrappers, thawed
- Oil for deep-fat frying
- Sweet chili sauce, optional

1. Toss the coleslaw mix, onions, soy sauce and sesame oil; let stand while cooking chicken. In a saucepan, bring 4 cups water to a boil. Reduce heat to maintain a simmer. Add chicken; cook, covered, until a thermometer inserted in chicken reads 165°, 15-20 minutes. Remove chicken; cool slightly. Finely chop chicken; toss with seasoned salt.
2. In a large bowl, mix cream cheese and chili sauce; stir in chicken and coleslaw mixture. With a corner of a spring roll wrapper facing you, place about 2 Tbsp. filling just below center of wrapper. (Cover remaining wrappers with a damp paper towel until ready to use.) Fold bottom corner over filling; moisten remaining edges with water. Fold side corners toward center over filling; roll up tightly, pressing tip to seal. Repeat.
3. In a cast-iron Dutch oven or electric skillet, heat oil to 375°. Fry spring rolls, a few at a time, until golden brown, 6-8 minutes, turning occasionally. Drain on paper towels. If desired, serve with sweet chili sauce.

FREEZE OPTION Freeze uncooked spring rolls in freezer containers, spacing them so they don't touch, and separating layers with waxed paper. To use, fry frozen spring rolls as directed, increasing time as necessary.

1 SPRING ROLL 186 cal., 14g fat (4g sat. fat), 30mg chol., 215mg sod., 10g carb. (1g sugars, 0 fiber), 6g pro.

SPICY BUTTERSCOTCH WINGS

We love big-time spicy chicken wings. I do a caramel sauce to balance the heat, but you could also glaze the wings with melted brown sugar.
—Aaron Salazar, Westminster, CO

PREP: 25 MIN. • **BAKE:** 25 MIN. • **MAKES:** 20 SERVINGS

- 2 lbs. chicken wings
- 2 Tbsp. soy sauce
- 2 Tbsp. ketchup
- 2 Tbsp. Sriracha chili sauce
- 1 tsp. pepper
- 1 tsp. crushed red pepper flakes
- 1 tsp. onion powder
- ½ tsp. salt

BUTTERSCOTCH SAUCE

- ½ cup sugar
- ½ cup 2% milk, warmed
- 2 Tbsp. butter

CRUMB TOPPING

- 1 Tbsp. butter
- ½ cup panko bread crumbs
- 2 green onions, sliced diagonally, divided
- 1 garlic clove, minced
- ½ tsp. salt
- ½ tsp. pepper
- 2 red bird's eye chili peppers, sliced, optional

1. Preheat oven to 400°. Using a sharp knife, cut through the 2 wing joints; discard wing tips. Combine next 7 ingredients; add wings and toss to coat.
2. Line a 15x10x1-in. pan with foil; spray with cooking spray. Bake wings in prepared pan 10 minutes; reduce heat to 350° and bake until juices run clear, 12-15 minutes. Remove from oven; keep warm.
3. Meanwhile, in a small skillet, spread the sugar; cook, without stirring, over medium heat until it begins to melt. Gently drag melted sugar to center of pan so it melts evenly. Cook, without stirring, until the melted sugar turns amber. Carefully stir in the warm milk and butter. Simmer, stirring frequently, 5-7 minutes or until thickened. Keep warm.
4. In a large skillet over medium heat, melt butter; add the bread crumbs, 1 green onion, garlic, salt and pepper. Cook and stir until bread crumbs are golden brown, about 2 minutes. Set aside.
5. To serve, toss the wings in butterscotch sauce. Sprinkle with crumb topping, remaining greer onion, and, if desired, sliced peppers. Serve hot.

1 PIECE 100 cal., 5g fat (2g sat. fat), 20mg chol., 312mg sod., 8g carb. (6g sugars, 0 fiber), 5g pro.

QUESO FUNDIDO

Dig in to this one-skillet dip with gooey cheese and a spicy kick from chorizo and pepper jack.
—Julie Merriman, Seattle, WA

PREP: 20 MIN. • **BAKE:** 15 MIN.
MAKES: 6 CUPS

- 1 lb. uncooked chorizo
- 2 cups fresh or frozen corn, thawed
- 1 large red onion, chopped
- 1 poblano pepper, chopped
- 8 oz. fresh goat cheese, crumbled
- 2 cups cubed Monterey Jack cheese
- 1 cup cubed pepper jack cheese
- 1 large tomato, seeded and chopped
- 3 green onions, thinly sliced
- Blue corn tortilla chips

1. Preheat oven to 350°. Crumble chorizo into a 10-in. cast-iron or other ovenproof skillet; add corn, red onion and pepper. Cook over medium heat until meat is fully cooked, 6-8 minutes; drain. Stir in the cheeses.
2. Bake until bubbly, 14-16 minutes. Sprinkle with tomato and green onions. Serve with chips.

¼ CUP 161 cal., 12g fat (6g sat. fat), 38mg chol., 365mg sod., 4g carb. (1g sugars, 1g fiber), 9g pro.

JALAPENO POPPER POCKET

For a fresh take on fried jalapeno poppers, we stuff chicken, cheeses and jalapenos inside puff pastry and bake.
—Sally Sibthorpe, Shelby Township, MI

PREP: 15 MIN.
BAKE: 20 MIN. + STANDING
MAKES: 12 SERVINGS

- 2 cups chopped rotisserie chicken (about 10 oz.)
- 1 carton (8 oz.) spreadable chive and onion cream cheese
- 1 cup shredded pepper jack or Monterey Jack cheese
- 1 can (4 oz.) diced jalapeno peppers
- 1 sheet frozen puff pastry, thawed
- 1 large egg, lightly beaten

1. Preheat oven to 425°. In a bowl, mix chicken, cream cheese, pepper jack cheese and peppers.
2. On a lightly floured surface, unfold puff pastry; roll into a 13-in. square. Place on a parchment-lined baking sheet. Spread half with chicken mixture to within ½ in. of edges. Fold remaining half over filling; press edges with a fork to seal.
3. Brush lightly with beaten egg. Cut slits in pastry. Bake 20-25 minutes or until golden brown. Let stand for 10 minutes before cutting.

1 PIECE 237 cal., 15g fat (6g sat. fat), 58mg chol., 252mg sod., 13g carb. (1g sugars, 2g fiber), 12g pro.

p. 28

Crowd-Pleasing Salads

LAYERED SALAD FOR A CROWD

This salad is a favorite with my three sons. I took it to a luncheon honoring our school district's food service manager, and she asked for the recipe! I like to make the dressing the day before so the flavors blend together.
—Linda Ashley, Leesburg, GA

TAKES: 20 MIN.
MAKES: 20 SERVINGS

- 1 cup mayonnaise
- ¼ cup 2% milk
- 2 tsp. dill weed
- ½ tsp. seasoning blend
- 1 bunch romaine, torn
- 2 medium carrots, grated
- 1 cup chopped red onion
- 1 medium cucumber, sliced
- 1 pkg. (10 oz.) frozen peas, thawed
- 1½ cups shredded cheddar cheese
- 8 bacon strips, cooked and crumbled

1. For dressing, in a small bowl, whisk the mayonnaise, milk, dill and seasoning blend.
2. In a 4-qt. clear glass serving bowl, layer the romaine, carrots, onion and cucumber (do not toss). Pour dressing over the top; sprinkle with peas, cheese and bacon. Cover and refrigerate until serving.

NOTE: This recipe was tested with Morton Nature's Seasons seasoning blend.

⅔ CUP 151 cal., 13g fat (4g sat. fat), 16mg chol., 216mg sod., 5g carb. (2g sugars, 1g fiber), 4g pro.

MINTY WATERMELON-CUCUMBER SALAD

Capturing the fantastic flavors of summer, this refreshing, beautiful salad will be the talk of any picnic or potluck.
—Roblynn Hunnisett, Guelph, ON

TAKES: 20 MIN. • **MAKES:** 16 SERVINGS

- 8 cups cubed seedless watermelon
- 2 English cucumbers, halved lengthwise and sliced
- 6 green onions, chopped
- ¼ cup minced fresh mint
- ¼ cup balsamic vinegar
- ¼ cup olive oil
- ½ tsp. salt
- ½ tsp. pepper

In a large bowl, combine the watermelon, cucumbers, green onions and mint. In a small bowl, whisk remaining ingredients. Pour over salad and toss to coat. Serve immediately or refrigerate, covered, up to 2 hours before serving.

¾ CUP 60 cal., 3g fat (0 sat. fat), 0 chol., 78mg sod., 9g carb. (8g sugars, 1g fiber), 1g pro.

HERB-VINAIGRETTE RED POTATOES

This is a great way to celebrate early produce from the garden. To add some more crunch, sprinkle with croutons.
—Debra Keil, Owasso, OK

PREP: 10 MIN. • **COOK:** 25 MIN. • **MAKES:** 12 SERVINGS

- 3 lbs. small red potatoes, quartered
- 1 lb. fresh asparagus, trimmed and cut into 2-in. pieces
- 2 cups sliced radishes
- 6 green onions, sliced
- 2 Tbsp. chopped fresh chives
- 2 Tbsp. chopped fresh parsley

VINAIGRETTE

- ¾ cup olive oil
- ¼ cup champagne vinegar or white vinegar
- 1 Tbsp. Dijon mustard
- ½ tsp. salt
- ¼ tsp. coarsely ground pepper

1. Place the potatoes in a large saucepan; add water to cover. Bring to a boil. Reduce the heat; cook, uncovered, 10-15 minutes or until tender. Remove potatoes with a slotted spoon; cool. Return water to a boil. Add the asparagus; cook, uncovered, 2-3 minutes or just until crisp-tender. Remove asparagus and immediately drop into ice water. Drain and pat dry.

2. Transfer potatoes and asparagus to a large bowl; add radishes, green onions and herbs. In a small bowl, whisk vinaigrette ingredients until blended. Pour over potato mixture; toss gently to coat. Serve at room temperature or chilled. Stir before serving.

¾ CUP 213 cal., 14g fat (2g sat. fat), 0 chol., 147mg sod., 20g carb. (2g sugars, 3g fiber), 3g pro.

EASY SUBSTITUTION

Add a bit of tang by replacing the champagne vinegar with apple cider vinegar.

STRAWBERRY KALE SALAD

This fresh, zingy salad is super easy and just like the one I get at Culver's! The sliced strawberries and mint give it an extra summery feel, and bacon and toasted almonds add the perfect amount of crunch.
—Luanne Asta, Hampton Bays, NY

TAKES: 25 MIN. • **MAKES:** 10 SERVINGS

- ½ cup olive oil
- ⅓ cup cider vinegar
- 1 tsp. honey
- ¼ tsp. salt
- ⅛ tsp. pepper
- 1 bunch kale (about 12 oz.), trimmed and chopped (about 14 cups)
- 2 cups sliced fresh strawberries
- ¾ lb. bacon strips, cooked and crumbled
- ¼ cup minced fresh mint
- 1 cup crumbled feta cheese
- ¼ cup slivered almonds, toasted

1. For dressing, whisk together the first 5 ingredients.
2. To serve, place chopped kale, strawberries, bacon and mint in a large bowl; toss with dressing. Sprinkle with cheese and almonds.

NOTE: To toast the nuts, bake in a shallow pan in a 350° oven for 5-10 minutes or cook in a skillet over low heat until lightly browned, stirring occasionally.

1⅓ CUPS 231 cal., 19g fat (4g sat. fat), 18mg chol., 399mg sod., 8g carb. (2g sugars, 2g fiber), 8g pro.

TANGY POPPY SEED FRUIT SALAD

For a fruit salad that's delightful, I combine berries and citrus with a honey lime dressing flecked with poppy seeds.
—Carrie Howell, Lehi, UT

TAKES: 20 MIN.
MAKES: 10 SERVINGS

- 1 can (20 oz.) unsweetened pineapple chunks, drained
- 1 lb. fresh strawberries, quartered
- 2 cups fresh blueberries
- 2 cups fresh raspberries
- 2 medium navel oranges, peeled and sectioned
- 2 medium kiwifruit, peeled, halved and sliced

DRESSING

- 2 to 4 Tbsp. honey
- ½ tsp. grated lime zest
- 2 Tbsp. lime juice
- 2 tsp. poppy seeds

Place all fruit in a large bowl. In a small bowl, whisk dressing ingredients. Drizzle over fruit; toss gently to combine.

⅔ CUP 117 cal., 1g fat (0 sat. fat), 0 chol., 3mg sod., 29g carb. (21g sugars, 5g fiber), 2g pro.

VIBRANT BLACK-EYED PEA SALAD

My black-eyed pea salad reminds me of a southern cooking class my husband and I took while visiting Savannah, Georgia. People go nuts for it at picnics and potlucks.
—Danielle Lee, Charleston, SC

PREP: 25 MIN. + CHILLING
MAKES: 10 SERVINGS

- 2 cans (15½ oz. each) black-eyed peas, rinsed and drained
- 2 cups grape tomatoes, halved
- 1 each small green, yellow and red peppers, finely chopped
- 1 small red onion, chopped
- 1 celery rib, chopped
- 2 Tbsp. minced fresh basil

DRESSING

- ¼ cup red wine vinegar or balsamic vinegar
- 1 Tbsp. stone-ground mustard
- 1 tsp. minced fresh oregano or ¼ tsp. dried oregano
- ¾ tsp. salt
- ½ tsp. freshly ground pepper
- ¼ cup olive oil

1. In a large bowl, combine peas, tomatoes, peppers, onion, celery and basil.
2. For dressing, in a small bowl, whisk vinegar, mustard, oregano, salt and pepper. Gradually whisk in oil until blended. Drizzle over salad; toss to coat. Refrigerate, covered, at least 3 hours before serving.

¾ CUP 130 cal., 6g fat (1g sat. fat), 0 chol., 319mg sod., 15g carb. (3g sugars, 3g fiber), 5g pro.

PATRIOTIC GELATIN SALAD

Almost as spectacular as the fireworks, this lovely salad makes quite a bang at patriotic celebrations. It's exciting to serve, and friends and family love the cool fruity and creamy layers.
—Sue Gronholz, Beaver Dam, WI

PREP: 20 MIN. + CHILLING • **MAKES:** 16 SERVINGS

- 2 pkg. (3 oz. each) berry blue gelatin
- 2 pkg. (3 oz. each) strawberry gelatin
- 4 cups boiling water, divided
- 2½ cups cold water, divided
- 2 envelopes unflavored gelatin
- 2 cups 2% milk
- 1 cup sugar
- 2 cups sour cream
- 2 tsp. vanilla extract

1. In 4 separate bowls, dissolve each package of gelatin in 1 cup boiling water. Add ½ cup cold water to each and stir. Pour 1 bowl of the blue gelatin into a 10-in. fluted tube pan coated with cooking spray; refrigerate until almost set, about 30 minutes.
2. Set the other 3 bowls of gelatin aside at room temperature. Soften unflavored gelatin in remaining cold water; let stand 5 minutes.
3. Heat the milk in a saucepan over medium heat just below boiling. Stir in softened gelatin and sugar until sugar is dissolved. Remove from heat; stir in sour cream and vanilla until smooth. When blue gelatin in pan is almost set, carefully spoon 1½ cups sour cream mixture over it. Refrigerate until almost set, about 30 minutes.
4. Carefully spoon 1 bowl of strawberry gelatin over cream layer. Refrigerate until almost set. Carefully spoon 1½ cups cream mixture over the strawberry layer. Refrigerate until almost set. Repeat, adding layers of blue gelatin, cream mixture and strawberry gelatin, refrigerating in between layers. Refrigerate several hours or overnight before serving.

NOTE This recipe takes time to prepare since each layer must be set before the next layer is added.

1 PIECE 206 cal., 7g fat (4g sat. fat), 23mg chol., 75mg sod., 34g carb. (33g sugars, 0 fiber), 5g pro.

"This was definitely the hit of my July 4th party! Although it takes time to make, it is definitely worth it. Followed the directions as written and it came out perfect!"
—JANETDEMETRES, TASTEOFHOME.COM

HONEYDEW & PROSCIUTTO SALAD

For parties, I turn melon and prosciutto into an easy salad with a honey mustard dressing. To add zip, stir in fresh basil and mint.
—*Julie Merriman, Seattle, WA*

TAKES: 30 MIN. • **MAKES:** 12 SERVINGS

- ⅓ cup olive oil
- ½ tsp. grated lime zest
- 2 Tbsp. lime juice
- 2 Tbsp. white wine vinegar
- 2 Tbsp. honey
- 1 tsp. Dijon mustard
- ¼ tsp. salt
- ¾ cup fresh cilantro leaves

SALAD

- 8 cups fresh arugula or baby spinach (about 5 oz.)
- ½ medium red onion, thinly sliced
- ¼ cup thinly sliced fresh mint leaves
- ¼ cup thinly sliced fresh basil leaves
- 8 cups diced honeydew melon
- 1 pkg. (8 oz.) fresh mozzarella cheese pearls
- ¼ lb. thinly sliced prosciutto, cut into wide strips

Place the first 8 ingredients in a blender; cover and process until smooth. Place arugula, onion and herbs in a large bowl. Drizzle with ⅓ cup vinaigrette and toss lightly to coat. In large serving bowl layer with a quarter of arugula mixture, honeydew, mozzarella cheese and prosciutto. Repeat layers 3 times. Serve with remaining vinaigrette.

1 SERVING 186 cal., 12g fat (4g sat. fat), 23mg chol., 294mg sod., 15g carb. (13g sugars, 1g fiber), 7g pro.

MACARONI COLESLAW

My friend Peggy brought this coleslaw to one of our picnics, and everyone liked it so much that we all had to have the recipe.
—Sandra Matteson, Westhope, ND

PREP: 25 MIN. + CHILLING
MAKES: 16 SERVINGS

- 1 pkg. (7 oz.) ring macaroni or ditalini
- 1 pkg. (14 oz.) coleslaw mix
- 2 medium onions, finely chopped
- 2 celery ribs, finely chopped
- 1 medium cucumber, finely chopped
- 1 medium green pepper, finely chopped
- 1 can (8 oz.) whole water chestnuts, drained and chopped

DRESSING

- 1½ cups Miracle Whip Light
- ⅓ cup sugar
- ¼ cup cider vinegar
- ½ tsp. salt
- ¼ tsp. pepper

1. Cook macaroni according to package directions; drain and rinse in cold water. Transfer to a large bowl; add the coleslaw mix, onions, celery, cucumber, green pepper and water chestnuts.
2. In a small bowl, whisk the dressing ingredients. Pour over salad; toss to coat. Cover and refrigerate for at least 1 hour.

¾ CUP 150 cal., 5g fat (1g sat. fat), 6mg chol., 286mg sod., 24g carb. (12g sugars, 2g fiber), 3g pro.

SUMMERTIME POTATO SALAD

Traditional potato salad gets fun flavor from sweet pickles and a hearty crunch from celery and radishes in this recipe. I'm especially fond of the creamy dressing.
—Ellen Benninger, Greenville, PA

PREP: 20 MIN. + CHILLING • **MAKES:** 10 SERVINGS

- 6 cups cubed peeled potatoes
- 4 hard-boiled large eggs, chopped
- 1 celery rib, chopped
- ½ cup chopped sweet pickles
- ⅓ cup chopped onion
- ⅓ cup chopped radishes
- ½ cup mayonnaise
- 3 Tbsp. sugar
- 1 Tbsp. white vinegar
- 1 Tbsp. 2% milk
- 1½ tsp. prepared mustard
- ½ tsp. salt
- Optional: Sliced green onions and paprika

1. Place potatoes in a saucepan and cover with water; bring to a boil. Reduce heat. Cook until tender, 10-15 minutes; drain. Place in a large bowl; add the eggs, celery, pickles, onion and radishes.
2. In a small bowl, combine the mayonnaise, sugar, vinegar, milk, mustard and salt; stir into potato mixture. Cover and refrigerate at least 1 hour before serving. If desired, garnish with onions and paprika.

¾ CUP 221 cal., 11g fat (2g sat. fat), 89mg chol., 297mg sod., 26g carb. (8g sugars, 2g fiber), 5g pro.

BOW TIE PASTA SALAD

This classic picnic pasta salad has it all. Fresh and bright cherry tomatoes, crisp red peppers, red onion and parsley are tossed with al dente bow tie pasta, salty olives, savory salami and provolone in a tangy homemade Italian dressing.
—Taste of Home *Test Kitchen*

TAKES: 30 MIN. + CHILLING • **MAKES:** 16 SERVINGS

- 1 lb. uncooked bow tie pasta
- 1 cup cherry tomatoes, halved
- ½ cup chopped red onion
- ½ cup cubed salami
- ⅓ cup cubed provolone cheese
- ¼ cup chopped sweet red pepper
- ¼ cup minced fresh parsley
- 1 can (2¼ oz.) sliced ripe olives, drained

DRESSING

- ¼ cup red wine vinegar
- 2 Tbsp. grated Parmesan cheese
- 1 Tbsp. Dijon mustard
- 2 garlic cloves, minced
- 2 tsp. Italian seasoning
- 1 tsp. salt
- ½ tsp. pepper
- ½ cup olive oil

1. Cook pasta according to package directions; drain. Transfer to a large bowl; stir in the tomatoes, onion, salami, provolone, red pepper, parsley and olives.

2. In a small bowl, whisk together vinegar, Parmesan, mustard, garlic, Italian seasoning, salt and pepper. Slowly drizzle with oil; whisk until combined. Drizzle dressing over pasta mixture and toss to coat. Cover and refrigerate until chilled, 1-2 hours.

¾ CUP 204 cal., 10g fat (2g sat. fat), 6mg chol., 326mg sod., 23g carb. (2g sugars, 1g fiber), 6g pro.

12-HOUR SALAD

This recipe was Mom's scrumptious scheme to get her kids to eat vegetables. She never had any trouble when she served this colorful crunchy salad. Mom thought this salad was a real bonus for the cook because it must be made the night before.
—Dorothy Bowen, Thomasville, NC

PREP: 20 MIN. + CHILLING
MAKES: 12 SERVINGS

- 8 cups torn mixed salad greens
- 1½ cups chopped celery
- 2 medium green peppers, chopped
- 1 medium red onion, chopped
- 2½ cups frozen peas (about 10 oz.), thawed
- 1 cup mayonnaise
- 1 cup sour cream
- 3 Tbsp. sugar
- 1 cup shredded cheddar cheese
- ½ lb. bacon strips, cooked and crumbled

1. Place greens in a 3-qt. bowl or 13x9-in. dish. Layer with celery, peppers, onion and peas.
2. Mix mayonnaise, sour cream and sugar; spread over top. Sprinkle with cheese and bacon. Refrigerate, covered, 12 hours or overnight.

1 CUP 280 cal., 23g fat (7g sat. fat), 22mg chol., 347mg sod., 11g carb. (6g sugars, 3g fiber), 8g pro.

CREAMY PINEAPPLE FLUFF SALAD

Guests of all ages will gravitate to this classic fluff salad packed with pineapple, marshmallows, chopped nuts and cherry bits.
—Janice Hensley, Owingsville, KY

TAKES: 25 MIN.
MAKES: 16 SERVINGS

- 1 pkg. (8 oz.) cream cheese, softened
- 1 can (14 oz.) sweetened condensed milk
- ¼ cup lemon juice
- 2 cans (20 oz.) pineapple tidbits, drained
- 1½ cups multicolored miniature marshmallows, divided
- 1 carton (8 oz.) frozen whipped topping, thawed
- ½ cup chopped nuts
- ⅓ cup maraschino cherries, chopped

In a large bowl, beat cream cheese, milk and lemon juice until smooth. Add pineapple tidbits and 1 cup marshmallows; fold in whipped topping. Sprinkle with chopped nuts and cherries and the remaining marshmallows. Refrigerate any leftovers.

½ CUP 161 cal., 10g fat (6g sat. fat), 16mg chol., 50mg sod., 17g carb. (12g sugars, 1g fiber), 2g pro.

QUICK & EASY

p. 37

Sensational Sides

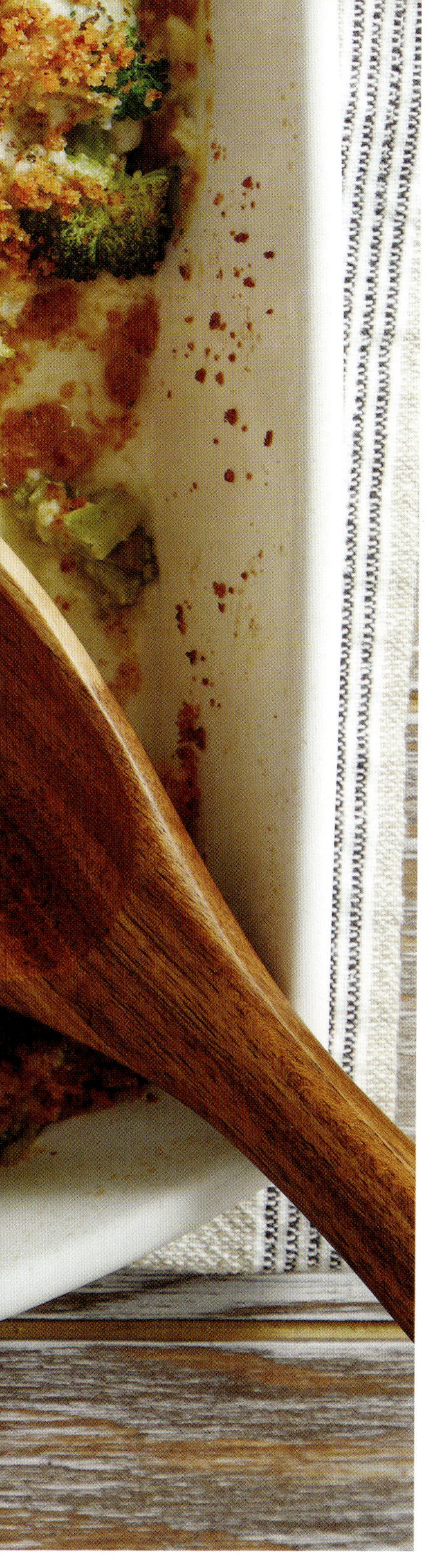

BAKED PARMESAN BROCCOLI

I began making this creamy side dish years ago as a way to get my kids to eat broccoli. They have since grown up but still request this satisfying casserole. It's truly a family favorite.
—Barbara Uhl, Wesley Chapel, FL

PREP: 30 MIN. • **BAKE:** 15 MIN. • **MAKES:** 12 SERVINGS

- 4 bunches broccoli, cut into florets
- 6 Tbsp. butter, divided
- 1 small onion, finely chopped
- 1 garlic clove, minced
- ¼ cup all-purpose flour
- 2 cups 2% milk
- 1 large egg yolk, beaten
- 1 cup grated Parmesan cheese
- ½ tsp. salt
- ⅛ tsp. pepper
- ½ cup seasoned bread crumbs

1. Preheat oven to 400°. Place half broccoli in a steamer basket; place basket in a large saucepan over 1 in. water. Bring to a boil; cover and steam 3-4 minutes or until crisp-tender. Place in a greased 13x9-in. baking dish; repeat with remaining broccoli.
2. Meanwhile, in a small saucepan over medium heat, melt 4 Tbsp. butter. Add onion; cook and stir until tender. Add garlic; cook 1 minute longer.
3. Stir in flour until blended; gradually add milk. Bring to a boil; cook and stir 2 minutes or until thickened. Stir a small amount of hot mixture into egg yolk; return all to the pan, stirring constantly. Cook and stir 1 minute longer. Remove from heat; stir in the cheese, salt and pepper. Pour over broccoli.
4. In a small skillet, cook bread crumbs in remaining butter until golden brown; sprinkle over the top.
5. Bake, uncovered, 15-18 minutes or until heated through.

¾ CUP 191 cal., 10g fat (5g sat. fat), 41mg chol., 388mg sod., 19g carb. (7g sugars, 6g fiber), 11g pro.

SUMMER RISOTTO

My mom always made this hearty dish to use up late summer garden vegetables. Often, I'll add sauteed mushrooms and serve it as an entrée with crusty bread and a salad.
—Shirley Hodge, Bangor, PA

PREP: 25 MIN. • **COOK:** 30 MIN. • **MAKES:** 12 SERVINGS

- 5½ to 6 cups reduced-sodium chicken broth
- 1 small onion, finely chopped
- 2 Tbsp. olive oil
- 1 Tbsp. butter
- 2 cups uncooked arborio rice
- 3 large tomatoes, chopped
- 2 cups fresh or frozen corn, thawed
- ½ cup crumbled feta cheese
- 2 Tbsp. minced fresh thyme or 2 tsp. dried thyme
- 2 Tbsp. minced fresh rosemary or 2 tsp. dried rosemary, crushed
- 2 Tbsp. minced fresh basil or 2 tsp. dried basil
- ¼ tsp. salt
- ¼ tsp. pepper
- Shredded Parmesan cheese

1. In a large saucepan, heat broth and keep warm. In a large skillet, saute onion in oil and butter until tender. Add rice; cook and stir for 2-3 minutes or until lightly browned. Stir in 1 cup of the warm broth. Cook and stir until all of the liquid is absorbed.
2. Add remaining broth, ½ cup at a time, stirring constantly. Allow the liquid to be absorbed between additions. Cook until risotto is creamy and rice is almost tender (total cooking time will be about 20 minutes).
3. Add the tomatoes, corn, feta cheese, herbs, salt and pepper; heat through. Sprinkle with Parmesan cheese. Serve immediately.

⅔ CUP 202 cal., 4g fat (2g sat. fat), 5mg chol., 366mg sod., 35g carb. (3g sugars, 2g fiber), 6g pro.

CORN WITH CILANTRO-LIME BUTTER

I like to use fresh cilantro from my garden in this lime butter I created especially for grilled corn.
—Andrea Reynolds, Westlake, OH

PREP: 15 MIN. + CHILLING
GRILL: 15 MIN.
MAKES: 12 SERVINGS

- ½ cup butter, softened
- ¼ cup minced fresh cilantro
- 1 Tbsp. lime juice
- 1½ tsp. grated lime zest
- 12 medium ears sweet corn, husked
- Grated Cotija cheese, optional

1. In a small bowl, mix butter, cilantro, lime juice and lime zest. Shape into a log; wrap in waxed paper. Refrigerate until firm, about 30 minutes. Wrap each ear of corn in a piece of heavy-duty foil (about 14 in. square).
2. Grill corn, covered, over medium heat until tender, turning occasionally, 15-20 minutes. Meanwhile, cut lime butter into 12 slices. Remove corn from grill. Carefully open foil, allowing steam to escape. Serve corn with butter and, if desired, cheese.

1 EAR OF CORN WITH 2 TSP. BUTTER
145 cal., 9g fat (5g sat. fat), 20mg chol., 67mg sod., 17g carb. (3g sugars, 2g fiber), 3g pro.

BEANS, BACON & TOMATO BAKE

For potlucks, I pull out the bacon, tomatoes and lima beans for a veggie-packed side that satisfies everyone.
—Karen Kumpulainen, Forest City, NC

PREP: 10 MIN. • **BAKE:** 35 MIN. • **MAKES:** 12 SERVINGS

- 8 bacon strips, cut into 1-in. pieces
- 1 cup finely chopped onion
- ⅔ cup finely chopped celery
- ½ cup finely chopped green pepper
- 2 garlic cloves, minced
- 2 tsp. all-purpose flour
- 2 tsp. sugar
- 2 tsp. salt
- ¼ tsp. pepper
- 2 cans (14½ oz. each) diced tomatoes, undrained
- 8 cups frozen lima beans (about 42 oz.), thawed

1. Preheat oven to 325°. In a 6-qt. stockpot, cook bacon, onion, celery and green pepper over medium heat until bacon is crisp and vegetables are tender. Add garlic; cook 1 minute longer. Stir in flour, sugar, salt and pepper. Add tomatoes. Bring to a boil, stirring constantly; cook and stir 1-2 minutes or until thickened. Stir in beans.
2. Transfer to a greased 3-qt. baking dish or a 13x9-in. baking pan. Bake, covered, 35-40 minutes or until beans are tender.

⅔ CUP 230 cal., 8g fat (3g sat. fat), 12mg chol., 666mg sod., 30g carb. (6g sugars, 9g fiber), 11g pro.

POTLUCK PAN ROLLS

The appealing homemade yeast-bread flavor of these golden rolls is unbeatable. Soft and light, they're great alongside any entree. Folks are disappointed if I don't bring them to potluck dinners.
—Carol Mead, Los Alamos, NM

PREP: 20 MIN. + RISING • **BAKE:** 20 MIN. • **MAKES:** 27 ROLLS

- 1 pkg. (¼ oz.) active dry yeast
- 1 tsp. plus ⅓ cup sugar, divided
- 1½ cups warm water (110° to 115°), divided
- ½ cup butter, melted
- 2 large eggs, room temperature
- ¼ cup instant nonfat dry milk powder
- 1¼ tsp. salt
- 5½ to 6 cups all-purpose flour

1. In a large bowl, dissolve yeast and 1 tsp. sugar in ½ cup water. Add the butter, eggs, milk powder, salt, 3 cups flour, and the remaining ⅓ cup sugar and 1 cup water. Beat on medium speed for 3 minutes. Stir in enough remaining flour to form a soft dough.
2. Turn onto a floured surface; knead until smooth and elastic, 6-8 minutes. Place in a greased bowl, turning once to grease top. Cover and let rise in a warm place until doubled, about 1½ hours.
3. Punch dough down. Divide into 27 pieces; shape into balls. Place 18 balls in a greased 13x9-in. baking pan and remaining balls in a greased 9-in. square baking pan. Cover and let rise until doubled, about 45 minutes.
4. Preheat oven to 375°. Bake rolls until golden brown, 17-20 minutes. Cool on wire racks.

1 ROLL 141 cal., 4g fat (1g sat. fat), 14mg chol., 158mg sod., 23g carb. (3g sugars, 1g fiber), 3g pro.

SLOW-COOKED CHEESY POTATOES

I like to fix a batch of these cheesy slow-cooker potatoes for potlucks and other big gatherings. Frozen hash browns, canned soup and flavored cream cheese make this wildly popular dish quick to put together.
—Julianne Henson, Streamwood, IL

PREP: 5 MIN. • **COOK:** 3½ HOURS • **MAKES:** 14 SERVINGS

- 1 pkg. (32 oz.) frozen cubed hash brown potatoes
- 1 can (10¾ oz.) condensed cream of potato soup, undiluted
- 2 cups shredded Colby-Monterey Jack cheese
- 1 cup sour cream
- ¼ tsp. pepper
- ⅛ tsp. salt
- 1 carton (8 oz.) spreadable chive and onion cream cheese

1. Place potatoes in a lightly greased 4-qt. slow cooker. In a large bowl, combine the soup, cheese, sour cream, pepper and salt. Pour over the potatoes and mix well.
2. Cover and cook on low until potatoes are tender, 3½-4 hours. Stir in cream cheese.

¾ CUP 214 cal., 13g fat (9g sat. fat), 42mg chol., 387mg sod., 17g carb. (2g sugars, 2g fiber), 6g pro.

Reader Review

"I fixed this for a potluck. Very simple, tasty and easy to transport. I will make it again!"
—FOOD3, TASTEOFHOME.COM

SLOW-COOKER CREAMED CORN WITH BACON

Every time I take this super rich corn to a potluck or work party, I leave with an empty slow cooker. It's decadent, homey and so worth the splurge.
—Melissa Pelkey Hass, Waleska, GA

PREP: 10 MIN. • **COOK:** 4 HOURS
MAKES: 20 SERVINGS

- 10 cups frozen corn (about 50 oz.), thawed
- 3 pkg. (8 oz. each) cream cheese, cubed
- ½ cup 2% milk
- ½ cup heavy whipping cream
- ½ cup butter, melted
- ¼ cup sugar
- 2 tsp. salt
- ¼ tsp. pepper
- 4 bacon strips, cooked and crumbled
- Chopped green onions

In a 5-qt. slow cooker, combine the first 8 ingredients. Cook, covered, on low 4-5 hours or until heated through. Stir just before serving. Sprinkle with bacon and green onions.

½ CUP 259 cal., 20g fat (11g sat. fat), 60mg chol., 433mg sod., 18g carb. (6g sugars, 1g fiber), 5g pro.

SLOW-COOKED POTATOES WITH SPRING ONIONS

I love the simplicity of this recipe, as well as the ease of preparation with my slow cooker. And everyone always likes roasted potatoes, even my pickiest child! If desired, top with shredded or crumbled cheese.
—Theresa Gomez, Stuart, FL

PREP: 5 MIN. • **COOK:** 6 HOURS • **MAKES:** 12 SERVINGS

- 4 lbs. small red potatoes
- 8 green onions, chopped (about 1 cup)
- 1 cup chopped sweet onion
- ¼ cup olive oil
- ½ tsp. salt
- ½ tsp. pepper

In a 5- or 6-qt. slow cooker, combine all ingredients. Cook, covered, on low until potatoes are tender, 6-8 hours.

1 SERVING 157 cal., 5g fat (1g sat. fat), 0 chol., 110mg sod., 26g carb. (2g sugars, 3g fiber), 3g pro.

FOURTH OF JULY BEAN CASSEROLE

The outstanding barbecue taste of these beans makes them a favorite for cookouts all summer and into the fall. It's a popular dish, even with kids. The beef makes it so much better than plain pork and beans.
—Donna Fancher, Lawrence, IN

PREP: 20 MIN. • **BAKE:** 1 HOUR • **MAKES:** 12 SERVINGS

- ½ lb. bacon strips, diced
- ½ lb. ground beef
- 1 cup chopped onion
- 1 can (28 oz.) pork and beans
- 1 can (16 oz.) kidney beans, rinsed and drained
- 1 can (15¼ oz.) lima beans, rinsed and drained
- ½ cup barbecue sauce
- ½ cup ketchup
- ½ cup sugar
- ½ cup packed brown sugar
- 2 Tbsp. prepared mustard
- 2 Tbsp. molasses
- 1 tsp. salt
- ½ tsp. chili powder

1. In a large skillet over medium heat, cook bacon, beef and onion until meat is no longer pink; drain.
2. Transfer to a greased 2½-qt. baking dish; add all beans and mix well. In a small bowl, combine the remaining ingredients; stir into beef and bean mixture.
3. Cover and bake at 350° for 45 minutes. Uncover; bake 15 minutes longer.

1 CUP 278 cal., 6g fat (2g sat. fat), 15mg chol., 933mg sod., 47g carb. (26g sugars, 7g fiber), 12g pro.

Reader Review

"My family and I love this recipe! I've taken it camping and to reunions and parties. Everyone asks me to share the recipe!"
—SULEWSKI, TASTEOFHOME.COM

BACON, CABBAGE & NOODLES

I received this recipe from a friend of Hungarian descent. Some folks turn up their noses when this is presented, but after one taste, they always come back for seconds...and thirds!
—Jeanie Castor, Decatur, IL

TAKES: 30 MIN.
MAKES: 12 SERVINGS

- 2 cups uncooked fine egg noodles
- ¾ lb. bacon strips, diced
- ½ medium head cabbage, thinly sliced
- ¼ tsp. salt
- Dash pepper

1. Cook egg noodles according to package directions. In a large skillet, cook bacon over medium heat until crisp. Using a slotted spoon, remove to paper towels; drain, reserving 3 Tbsp. drippings.
2. Add cabbage to drippings; cover and cook on low for 20 minutes or until cabbage is tender, stirring occasionally. Drain noodles. Stir into skillet. Add bacon, salt and pepper; heat through.

¾ CUP 112 cal., 10g fat (3g sat. fat), 20mg chol., 244mg sod., 7g carb. (1g sugars, 1g fiber), 5g pro.

SLOW-COOKER PEAS & CARROTS

The classic combination of peas and carrots is made even better with a few simple flavor enhancers. Slow-cooking allows the ingredients to meld for maximum richness.
—Theresa Kreyche, Tustin, CA

PREP: 15 MIN. • **COOK:** 5¼ HOURS
MAKES: 12 SERVINGS

- 1 lb. carrots, sliced
- 1 large onion, chopped
- ¼ cup water
- ¼ cup butter, cubed
- ¼ cup honey
- 4 garlic cloves, minced
- 1 tsp. salt
- 1 tsp. dried marjoram
- ⅛ tsp. white pepper
- 1 pkg. (16 oz.) frozen peas

In a 3-qt. slow cooker, combine the first 9 ingredients. Cook, covered, on low 5 hours. Stir in peas. Cook, covered, on high 15-25 minutes longer or until vegetables are tender.

½ CUP 106 cal., 4g fat (2g sat. fat), 10mg chol., 293mg sod., 16g carb. (10g sugars, 3g fiber), 3g pro.

CORNBREAD PUDDING

I love serving this satisfying corn bread pudding recipe with shrimp or other seafood. I actually adapted the dish from my mom's recipe, and it always reminds me of her.
—Bob Gebhardt, Wausau, WI

PREP: 5 MIN. • **BAKE:** 40 MIN. • **MAKES:** 12 SERVINGS

- 2 large eggs
- 1 cup sour cream
- 1 can (15¼ oz.) whole kernel corn, drained
- 1 can (14¾ oz.) cream-style corn
- ½ cup butter, melted
- 1 pkg. (8½ oz.) cornbread/muffin mix
- ¼ tsp. paprika

1. In a large bowl, combine the first 5 ingredients. Stir in cornbread mix just until blended. Pour into a greased 3-qt. baking dish. Sprinkle with paprika.
2. Bake, uncovered, at 350° for 40-45 minutes or until a knife inserted in the center comes out clean. Serve warm.

1 SERVING 249 cal., 14g fat (8g sat. fat), 73mg chol., 461mg sod., 26g carb. (8g sugars, 1g fiber), 4g pro.

SPINACH BALLS

This is delicious for a potluck side dish or appetizer. And since it can be made ahead, you might think about doubling the recipe and freezing some for unexpected guests.
—Faye Buffenmeyer, Lebanon, PA

TAKES: 20 MIN. • **MAKES:** ABOUT 4 DOZEN

- 1 pkg. (10 oz.) frozen chopped spinach
- 2½ cups herb-seasoned stuffing mix
- 1 medium onion, finely chopped
- 3 large eggs, beaten
- ¼ cup grated Parmesan cheese
- 6 Tbsp. butter, melted
- ½ tsp. garlic salt
- ¼ tsp. pepper

Cook spinach according to package directions; drain well, squeezing out excess liquid. In a large bowl, combine spinach with remaining ingredients. Shape mixture into 1-in. balls; place on an ungreased baking sheet. Bake at 350° for 10 minutes or until very lightly browned.

1 SPINACH BALL62 cal., 2g fat (1g sat. fat), 16mg chol., 209mg sod., 8g carb. (1g sugars, 0g fiber), 2g pro.

MAKE-AHEAD GREATS

These Spinach Balls can be assembled ahead of time and simply refrigerated overnight before baking.

QUICK
& EASY

CREOLE CORNBREAD

Cornbread is a staple of Cajun and Creole cuisine. This version is an old favorite, and it really tastes wonderful. I found the recipe in the bottom of my recipe drawer.
—Enid Hebert, Lafayette, LA

PREP: 15 MIN. • **BAKE:** 45 MIN. • **MAKES:** 12 SERVINGS

- 2 cups cooked rice
- 1 cup yellow cornmeal
- ½ cup chopped onion
- 1 to 2 Tbsp. seeded chopped jalapeno pepper
- 1 tsp. salt
- ½ tsp. baking soda
- 2 large eggs, room temperature
- 1 cup 2% milk
- ¼ cup canola oil
- 1 can (16½ oz.) cream-style corn
- 3 cups shredded cheddar cheese
- Additional cornmeal

1. In a large bowl, combine rice, 1 cup cornmeal, onion, peppers, salt and baking soda.
2. In another bowl, beat eggs, milk and oil. Add corn; mix well. Stir into rice mixture until blended. Fold in cheese. Sprinkle a well-greased 10-in. ovenproof skillet with cornmeal. Pour batter into skillet.
3. Bake at 350° for 45-50 minutes or until a toothpick inserted in the bread comes out clean. Cut into wedges and serve warm.

NOTE Wear disposable gloves when cutting hot peppers; the oils can burn skin. Avoid touching your face.

1 PIECE 272 cal., 14g fat (7g sat. fat), 68mg chol., 551mg sod., 26g carb. (3g sugars, 2g fiber), 10g pro.

"I made this several times; once for a BBQ contest. I placed second with it!"
—PUGSLEY61, TASTEOFHOME.COM

POTLUCK MAC & CHEESE

Bacon and jalapeno upgrade ordinary macaroni and cheese, giving it great grown-up taste. I serve this dish throughout the year.
—Shelly Boehm, South Bend, IN

PREP: 35 MIN. • **BAKE:** 40 MIN. • **MAKES:** 16 SERVINGS (¾ CUP EACH)

- 6 cups uncooked elbow macaroni
- 1 lb. bacon strips, chopped
- 1 jalapeno pepper, seeded and minced
- 3 cups 2% milk
- 2 cups shredded pepper Jack cheese
- 1 pkg. (8 oz.) Velveeta, cubed
- 1 cup shredded Colby-Monterey Jack cheese
- 1 cup shredded cheddar cheese
- 1 tsp. onion powder
- 1 tsp. chili powder
- ½ tsp. salt
- ½ tsp. pepper
- Dash hot pepper sauce
- 3 green onions, chopped

1. Cook macaroni according to package directions.
2. Meanwhile, in a Dutch oven, cook bacon over medium heat until crisp. Using a slotted spoon, remove to paper towels; drain, reserving 1 Tbsp. drippings. Saute jalapeno in reserved drippings. Add milk and cheeses to pan; cook and stir until blended. Stir in the onion powder, chili powder, salt, pepper and pepper sauce.
3. Drain macaroni; add to the pan with the onions and cooked bacon. Mix well.
4. Transfer to a greased 13x9-in. baking dish. Cover and bake at 350° for 30 minutes. Uncover; bake 10-15 minutes longer or until heated through.

NOTE Wear disposable gloves when cutting hot peppers; the oils can burn skin. Avoid touching your face.

¾ CUP 438 cal., 26g fat (13g sat. fat), 75mg chol., 1106mg sod., 26g carb. (4g sugars, 1g fiber), 25g pro.

BAKED TWO-CHEESE GRITS

To a Southerner, grits are a true staple. Combine them with bacon and cheese, and even Northerners will be asking for a second helping.
—Melissa Rogers, Tuscaloosa, AL

PREP: 25 MIN. • **BAKE:** 40 MIN. + STANDING • **MAKES:** 12 SERVINGS

- **6 thick-sliced bacon strips, chopped**
- **3 cups water**
- **3 cups chicken stock**
- **1 tsp. garlic powder**
- **½ tsp. pepper**
- **2 cups quick-cooking grits**
- **12 oz. Velveeta, cubed (about 2⅓ cups)**
- **½ cup butter, cubed**
- **½ cup 2% milk**
- **4 large eggs, lightly beaten**
- **2 cups shredded white cheddar cheese**

1. Preheat oven to 350°. In a large saucepan, cook the bacon over medium heat until crisp, stirring occasionally. Remove pan from heat. Remove bacon with a slotted spoon; drain on paper towels.
2. Add water, stock, garlic powder and pepper to bacon drippings; bring to a boil. Slowly stir in grits. Reduce heat to medium-low; cook, covered, 5-7 minutes or until thickened, stirring occasionally. Remove from heat.
3. Add Velveeta and butter; stir until melted. Stir in milk. Slowly stir in eggs until blended. Transfer to a greased 13x9-in. baking dish. Sprinkle with bacon and shredded cheese. Bake, uncovered, 40-45 minutes or until edges are golden brown and cheese is melted. Let stand 10 minutes before serving.

FREEZE OPTION Cool unbaked casserole; cover and freeze. To use, partially thaw in refrigerator overnight. Remove casserole from refrigerator 30 minutes before baking. Bake grits as directed, increasing time to 50-60 minutes or until heated through and a thermometer inserted in center reads 165°.

¾ CUP 466 cal., 34g fat (18g sat. fat), 143mg chol., 840mg sod., 23g carb. (3g sugars, 1g fiber), 17g pro.

p. 58

Make & Take Mains

ONE-POT BACON CHEESEBURGER PASTA

When we don't want to fire up the grill for burgers, I whip up a big pot of this cheesy pasta. Believe it or not, it tastes just like a bacon cheeseburger, and it's much easier for my young children to enjoy.
—Carly Terrell, Granbury, TX

PREP: 15 MIN. • **COOK:** 35 MIN. • **MAKES:** 12 SERVINGS

- 8 bacon strips, chopped
- 2 lbs. ground beef
- ½ large red onion, chopped
- 12 oz. uncooked spiral pasta
- 4 cups chicken broth
- 2 cans (15 oz. each) crushed tomatoes
- 1 can (8 oz.) tomato sauce
- 1 cup water
- ¼ cup ketchup
- 3 Tbsp. prepared mustard
- 2 Tbsp. Worcestershire sauce
- ¼ tsp. salt
- ¼ tsp. pepper
- 2 cups shredded cheddar cheese, divided
- ⅓ cup chopped dill pickle
- Optional: Chopped tomatoes, shredded lettuce, sliced pickles and sliced red onion

1. In a 6-qt. stockpot, cook bacon over medium heat, stirring occasionally, until crisp, 6-8 minutes. Remove with a slotted spoon; drain on paper towels. Discard drippings.
2. In the same pot, cook ground beef and onion over medium heat, crumbling beef, until meat is no longer pink, 6-8 minutes; drain. Add the next 10 ingredients; bring to a boil. Reduce heat; simmer, covered, until pasta is al dente, stirring occasionally, about 10 minutes.
3. Stir in 1 cup cheese, the pickle and the bacon; cook and stir until cheese is melted. Serve with remaining 1 cup cheese and, if desired, tomatoes, lettuce, pickles and red onion.

1⅓ CUPS 390 cal., 18g fat (8g sat. fat), 73mg chol., 1023mg sod., 31g carb. (7g sugars, 3g fiber), 25g pro.

TEST KITCHEN TIP

Take the extra time and shred cheese from a block for this recipe; it will stir in with a smoother texture than pre-shredded cheese.

SLOW-SIMMERED BEEF BURRITOS

Recipes that are leaner in fat and calories—like this one for beef burritos—helped me lose 30 pounds! The meat is so tender and delicious.
—Shirley Davidson, Thornton, CO

PREP: 20 MIN. • **COOK:** 8 HOURS • **MAKES:** 2 DOZEN

- 2 beef sirloin tip roasts (3 lbs. each)
- 4 cans (4 oz. each) chopped green chiles
- 1 medium onion, chopped
- 3 medium jalapeno peppers, seeded and chopped
- 3 garlic cloves, sliced
- 3 tsp. chili powder
- 1½ tsp. ground cumin
- 1 tsp. salt-free seasoning blend, optional
- 1 cup reduced-sodium beef broth
- 24 fat-free flour tortillas (8 in.), warmed
- Optional: Chopped tomatoes, shredded lettuce and shredded reduced-fat cheddar cheese

1. Trim fat from roasts; cut meat into large chunks. Place in a 5- or 6-qt. slow cooker. Top with the chiles, onion, jalapenos, garlic, chili powder, cumin and, if desired, seasoning blend. Pour broth over all. Cover and cook on low for 8-9 hours or until meat is tender.
2. Remove beef; cool slightly. Shred with 2 forks. Cool cooking liquid slightly; skim off fat. In a blender, cover and process cooking liquid in small batches until smooth.
3. Return liquid and beef to slow cooker; heat through. Place ⅓ cup beef mixture on each tortilla. Top with tomatoes, lettuce and cheese as desired. Fold in ends and sides of tortillas.

NOTE Wear disposable gloves when cutting hot peppers; the oils can burn skin. Avoid touching your face.

1 BURRITO 262 cal., 5g fat (2g sat. fat), 72mg chol., 376mg sod., 26g carb. (0 sugars, 2g fiber), 26g pro.

POTLUCK FRIED CHICKEN

This Sunday dinner staple is first fried and then baked to a crispy golden brown. Well-seasoned with oregano and sage, this classic is sure to satisfy diners at church potlucks or late-summer picnics too. I love fixing it for family and friends.
—Donna Kuhaupt, Slinger, WI

PREP: 40 MIN. • **BAKE:** 25 MIN. • **MAKES:** 12 SERVINGS

- 1½ cups all-purpose flour
- ½ cup cornmeal
- ¼ cup cornstarch
- 3 tsp. salt
- 2 tsp. paprika
- 1 tsp. dried oregano
- 1 tsp. rubbed sage
- 1 tsp. pepper
- 2 large eggs
- ¼ cup water
- 2 broiler/fryer chickens (3 to 4 lbs. each), cut up
- Oil for frying

1. In a large shallow dish, combine flour, cornmeal, cornstarch, salt, paprika, oregano, sage and pepper. In a shallow bowl, beat eggs and water. Dip chicken into egg mixture; place in flour mixture, a few pieces at a time, and turn to coat.
2. In an electric skillet, heat 1 in. oil to 375°. Fry chicken, a few pieces at a time, until golden and crispy, 3-5 minutes on each side.
3. Place in 2 ungreased 15x10x1-in. baking pans. Bake, uncovered, at 350° until juices run clear, 25-30 minutes.

5 OZ. COOKED CHICKEN 497 cal., 29g fat (6g sat. fat), 135mg chol., 693mg sod., 20g carb. (0 sugars, 1g fiber), 36g pro.

"My family loves this fried chicken recipe! When we have made it for my kid's friends or for gatherings, the recipe is always requested."
—DEB, TASTEOFHOME.COM

LAYERED PICNIC LOAVES

This big sandwich is inspired by one I fell in love with at a New York deli. It's easy to make ahead of time and cart to any party. Kids and adults alike say it's super.
—*Marion Lowery, Medford, OR*

PREP: 20 MIN. + CHILLING • **MAKES:** 2 LOAVES (12 SERVINGS EACH)

- 2 unsliced loaves (1 lb. each) Italian bread
- ¼ cup olive oil
- 3 garlic cloves, minced
- 2 tsp. Italian seasoning, divided
- ½ lb. deli roast beef
- 12 slices part-skim mozzarella cheese (1 oz. each)
- 16 fresh basil leaves
- 3 medium tomatoes, thinly sliced
- ¼ lb. thinly sliced salami
- 1 jar (6½ oz.) marinated artichoke hearts, drained and sliced
- 1 pkg. (10 oz.) ready-to-serve salad greens
- 8 oz. thinly sliced deli chicken
- 1 medium onion, thinly sliced
- ¼ tsp. salt
- ⅛ tsp. pepper

1. Cut loaves in half horizontally; hollow out tops and bottoms, leaving ½-in. shells (discard the removed bread or save it for another use).
2. Combine oil and garlic; brush inside bread shells. Sprinkle with 1 tsp. Italian seasoning. Layer bottom of each loaf with a fourth of each: roast beef, mozzarella, basil, tomatoes, salami, artichokes, salad greens, chicken and onion. Repeat layers. Season with salt, pepper and remaining Italian seasoning.
3. Drizzle with remaining oil mixture if desired. Replace bread tops; wrap tightly and refrigerate at least 1 hour before slicing.

1 PIECE 341 cal., 18g fat (7g sat. fat), 47mg chol., 991mg sod., 26g carb. (3g sugars, 2g fiber), 19g pro.

PIZZA ROLL-UPS

This has been a regular after-school snack in my house since I first got the recipe through my 4-H club. These bite-sized pizza treats, made with refrigerated crescent rolls, are especially good served with spaghetti sauce for dipping.
—Donna Klettke, Wheatland, MO

PREP: 20 MIN. • **BAKE:** 15 MIN.
MAKES: 2 DOZEN

- ½ lb. ground beef
- 1 can (8 oz.) tomato sauce
- ½ cup shredded part-skim mozzarella cheese
- ½ tsp. dried oregano
- 2 tubes (8 oz. each) refrigerated crescent rolls

1. In a large skillet, cook and crumble beef over medium heat until no longer pink; drain. Remove from the heat. Add the tomato sauce, mozzarella cheese and oregano.
2. Separate crescent dough into 8 rectangles, pinching seams together. Place about 3 Tbsp. of meat mixture along 1 long side of each rectangle. Roll up, jelly-roll style, starting with the long side lined with filling. Cut each roll into 3 pieces.
3. Place, seam side down, 2 in. apart on greased baking sheets. Bake at 375° for 15 minutes or until golden brown.

1 ROLL-UP 94 cal., 5g fat (1g sat. fat), 7mg chol., 206mg sod., 9g carb. (2g sugars, 0 fiber), 4g pro.

SLOW-SIMMERED SAUSAGES

This recipe has become a regular at our church potlucks. Let's just say I'm in trouble if I show up at a get-together and they don't appear! For a fun dinner spin, try these sausage and kraut sandwiches over mashed potatoes.
—Patsy Unruh, Perryton, TX

PREP: 20 MIN. • **COOK:** 4 HOURS • **MAKES:** 12 SANDWICHES

- 2 cans (14½ oz. each) no-salt-added diced tomatoes, drained
- 2 cans (14 oz. each) sauerkraut, rinsed and drained
- ½ lb. sliced fresh mushrooms
- 1 large sweet pepper, thinly sliced
- 1 large onion, halved and thinly sliced
- 2 Tbsp. brown sugar
- ½ tsp. pepper
- 2 pkg. (14 oz. each) smoked sausage, sliced
- 12 pretzel sausage buns, warmed and split partway

1. In a 5- or 6-qt. slow cooker, combine first 7 ingredients. In a large skillet, saute sausage over medium-high heat until lightly browned. Stir into tomato mixture.
2. Cook, covered, on low 4-5 hours, until vegetables are tender. Serve in buns.

1 SANDWICH 468 cal., 23g fat (8g sat. fat), 44mg chol., 1491mg sod., 51g carb. (12g sugars, 4g fiber), 17g pro.

SLOPPY JOE UNDER A BUN

I usually keep a can of sloppy joe sauce in the pantry because our kids love sloppy joes. But I don't always have buns on hand. With this fun casserole, we can enjoy the flavors they adore anytime.
—Trish Bloom, Ray, MI

PREP: 15 MIN. • **BAKE:** 25 MIN.
MAKES: 8 SERVINGS

- 1½ lbs. ground beef
- 1 can (15½ oz.) sloppy joe sauce
- 2 cups shredded cheddar cheese
- 2 cups biscuit/baking mix
- 2 large eggs, room temperature, lightly beaten
- 1 cup 2% milk
- 1 Tbsp. sesame seeds

1. In a large skillet, cook and crumble beef over medium heat until no longer pink; drain. Stir in sloppy joe sauce. Transfer to a lightly greased 13x9-in. baking dish; sprinkle with cheese.
2. In a large bowl, combine biscuit mix, eggs and milk just until blended. Pour over cheese; sprinkle with sesame seeds. Bake, uncovered, at 400° for 25 minutes or until golden brown.

1 SERVING 423 cal., 23g fat (12g sat. fat), 129mg chol., 961mg sod., 26g carb. (6g sugars, 1g fiber), 27g pro.

JIMMY'S BANG BANG CHICKEN SLIDERS

I simmer chicken thighs in a spicy-sweet sauce, shred them and then pile 'em high on pretzel buns to create an incredibly addictive party food.
—James Schend, Pleasant Prairie, WI

PREP: 45 MIN. • **BAKE:** 10 MIN. • **MAKES:** 1 DOZEN

- 3 lbs. boneless skinless chicken thighs
- 3 Tbsp. olive oil, divided
- ½ cup ketchup
- ½ cup Sriracha chili sauce
- ½ cup plus 2 Tbsp. honey, divided
- ½ cup water
- 3 Tbsp. lime juice
- 2 tsp. grated lime zest
- 2 tsp. minced garlic
- 1 tsp. ground ginger
- ¼ tsp. pepper
- 12 mini pretzel buns, split
- 12 slices part-skim mozzarella cheese, halved
- ¼ to ½ tsp. crushed red pepper flakes
- Coarse salt, optional
- 2 green onions, chopped

SRIRACHA-LIME DIPPING SAUCE

- 1 cup reduced-fat mayonnaise
- 2 Tbsp. Sriracha chili sauce
- 2 Tbsp. lime juice
- 2 tsp. grated lime zest

1. In a Dutch oven over medium heat, brown chicken in 1 Tbsp. olive oil for 5 minutes.
2. Meanwhile, stir together ketchup, chili sauce, ½ cup honey, water, lime juice and zest, garlic, ginger and pepper. Pour over browned chicken and bring to a boil. Reduce heat to low and cook, covered, stirring occasionally, until chicken is tender, 25-30 minutes. Remove chicken and bring sauce back to a simmer; cook until thick, about 5 minutes. Shred chicken with 2 forks; toss with reduced sauce.
3. Preheat oven to 375°. Place bottom buns in a greased 13x9-in. baking dish. Place half a slice of cheese on each of the buns; spoon chicken mixture on top of cheese. Top with remaining cheese; replace the bun tops. Stir together the remaining 2 Tbsp. olive oil, remaining 2 Tbsp. honey and the red pepper flakes. Brush over bun tops. Sprinkle with the coarse salt if desired.
4. Bake until tops are golden and cheese has melted, 10-15 minutes. Garnish with green onions.
5. Stir together all sauce ingredients. Serve alongside sliders.

1 SLIDER 516 cal., 26g fat (7g sat. fat), 100mg chol., 892mg sod., 40g carb. (18g sugars, 1g fiber), 31g pro.

BREAKFAST EMPANADAS

I take one Saturday per month and prepare many make-ahead meals. These breakfast empanadas are among my family's favorites, and they freeze easily for busy mornings. You can add chopped jalapenos when cooking the eggs if you prefer a spicy filling.
—Marina Castle Kelley, Canyon Country, CA

PREP: 45 MIN. + CHILLING • **COOK:** 5 MIN./BATCH • **MAKES:** 2½ DOZEN

- ½ lb. fresh chorizo or bulk pork sausage
- 9 large eggs, divided use
- 2 cups frozen shredded hash brown potatoes
- 1 cup shredded mozzarella cheese
- ½ cup shredded sharp cheddar cheese
- ¼ tsp. salt
- ¼ tsp. pepper
- ⅛ tsp. garlic powder
- 3 pkg. (14 oz. each) frozen empanada dough disks, thawed
- Oil for deep-fat frying
- Optional: Salsa verde, sour cream and sliced avocado

1. In a large skillet, cook chorizo over medium heat until cooked through, 6-8 minutes, breaking into crumbles; drain and set aside. Return pan to stove.
2. In a large bowl, whisk 8 eggs. Add to skillet; cook and stir over medium heat until the eggs are thickened and no liquid egg remains. Transfer to a large bowl. Stir in chorizo, hash browns, cheeses, salt, pepper and garlic powder.
3. Beat remaining egg; brush over edges of dough disks. Place 3 Tbsp. filling on 1 side of each disk. Fold dough over filling. Pinch edges and press to seal. Refrigerate for 30 minutes.
4. In an electric skillet or deep-fat fryer, heat oil to 375°. Fry the empanadas, a few at a time, until golden brown, 3-4 minutes, turning occasionally. Drain on paper towels. If desired, sprinkle with additional salt. Serve with salsa verde, sour cream and avocado if desired.

FREEZE OPTION Cover and freeze uncooked empanadas on waxed paper-lined baking sheets until firm. Transfer to freezer containers; return to freezer. To use, cover and thaw overnight in refrigerator in a single layer. Fry as directed, increasing time if necessary.

1 EMPANADA 218 cal., 12g fat (4g sat. fat), 67mg chol., 304mg sod., 21g carb. (0 sugars, 1g fiber), 9g pro.

BEEF BOLOGNESE WITH LINGUINE

After much research, tasting and tweaking, I finally came up with this recipe, based on a dish from an Italian restaurant where I worked. It's perfect for feeding a house full of guests.
—Christine Wendland, Browns Mills, NJ

PREP: 30 MIN. • **COOK:** 3½ HOURS • **MAKES:** 18 SERVINGS

- 3 lbs. lean ground beef (90% lean)
- ⅓ cup olive oil
- 3 medium onions, chopped
- 3 large carrots, chopped
- 6 celery ribs, chopped
- 1 can (12 oz.) tomato paste, divided
- 9 garlic cloves, sliced
- 3 Tbsp. dried parsley flakes
- 5 tsp. kosher salt
- 3 tsp. dried basil
- 3 tsp. dried marjoram
- 1½ tsp. coarsely ground pepper
- ¼ tsp. crushed red pepper flakes
- 1½ cups dry red wine
- 3 cans (28 oz. each) diced tomatoes, undrained
- 1½ cups beef stock
- 6 bay leaves
- 3 cups 2% milk
- ¾ cup grated Parmesan cheese
- Hot cooked linguine

1. In a stockpot, cook half the beef over medium heat until no longer pink, breaking into crumbles, 8-10 minutes. Remove beef with a slotted spoon; set aside. Pour off drippings. Repeat with remaining beef.

2. In the same stockpot, heat oil over medium heat. Add onions, carrots and celery; cook and stir until tender. Stir in 1 cup tomato paste; cook and stir 3 minutes longer. Add garlic, seasonings and beef.

3. Stir in wine. Bring to a boil; cook until liquid is almost evaporated. Add tomatoes, stock and bay leaves; return to a boil. Reduce heat; simmer, uncovered, until desired consistency, about 3 hours, stirring in milk halfway through cooking.

4. Remove bay leaves. Stir in cheese and remaining tomato paste; heat through. Serve with linguine and, if desired, additional cheese.

1 CUP 269 cal., 12g fat (4g sat. fat), 53mg chol., 938mg sod., 17g carb. (10g sugars, 4g fiber), 20g pro.

POTLUCK HOT DISH

This recipe was in my mother's church cookbook, and now it's in my church cookbook! Apparently it was too good to miss a generation. I often make this dish to take along to potlucks.
—Norma Turner, Haslett, MI

PREP: 40 MIN. • **BAKE:** 30 MIN. • **MAKES:** 8 SERVINGS

- 1 lb. ground beef
- 2 cups sliced peeled potatoes
- 2 cups finely chopped celery
- ¾ cup finely chopped carrots
- ¼ cup finely chopped green pepper
- ¼ cup finely chopped onion
- 2 Tbsp. butter
- 1 cup water
- 2 cans (10¾ oz. each) condensed cream of mushroom soup, undiluted
- 1 can (5 oz.) chow mein noodles, divided
- 1 cup shredded cheddar cheese

1. Preheat oven to 350°. In a large skillet, cook and crumble beef over medium heat until no longer pink; drain and set aside.
2. In same skillet, saute potatoes, celery, carrots, green pepper and onion in butter 5 minutes. Add water; cover and simmer 10 minutes or until vegetables are tender. Stir in soup and cooked ground beef until blended.
3. Sprinkle half the chow mein noodles into a greased shallow 2-qt. baking dish. Spoon meat mixture over noodles. Cover and bake 20 minutes. Top with cheese and remaining noodles. Bake, uncovered, 10 minutes longer or until heated through.

1 SERVING 339 cal., 20g fat (9g sat. fat), 53mg chol., 537mg sod., 25g carb. (2g sugars, 3g fiber), 16g pro.

SLOW-COOKED TURKEY WITH BERRY COMPOTE

This delicious dish gives you that yummy turkey flavor without taking up oven space. The berries make a perfect chutney any time of year. For a browner turkey, broil it for a few minutes before serving.
—Margaret Bracher, Robertsdale, AL

PREP: 35 MIN. • **COOK:** 3 HRS + STANDING
MAKES: 12 SERVINGS (3¼ CUPS COMPOTE)

- 1 tsp. salt
- ½ tsp. garlic powder
- ½ tsp. dried thyme
- ½ tsp. pepper
- 2 boneless turkey breast halves (2 lbs. each)
- ⅓ cup water

COMPOTE

- 2 medium apples, peeled and finely chopped
- 2 cups fresh raspberries
- 2 cups fresh blueberries
- 1 cup white grape juice
- ¼ tsp. crushed red pepper flakes
- ¼ tsp. ground ginger

1. Mix salt, garlic powder, thyme and pepper; rub over turkey breasts. Place in a 5- or 6-qt. slow cooker. Pour water around turkey. Cook, covered, on low 3-4 hours (a thermometer inserted in turkey should read at least 165°).
2. Remove turkey from slow cooker; tent with foil. Let stand 10 minutes before slicing.
3. Meanwhile, in a large saucepan, combine compote ingredients. Bring to a boil. Reduce heat to medium; cook, uncovered, stirring occasionally, until mixture is slightly thickened and apples are tender, 15-20 minutes. Serve turkey with compote.

5 OZ. COOKED TURKEY WITH ¼ CUP COMPOTE 215 cal., 1g fat (0 sat. fat), 94mg chol., 272mg sod., 12g carb. (8g sugars, 2g fiber), 38g pro.

Reader Review

"Yummy! Very simple to put together and then let the slow cooker take care of the rest. The berry compote was also very good. The crushed red pepper flakes give it just enough heat."
—APSCHWARTZ, TASTEOFHOME.COM

SLOW-COOKER SPIRAL HAM

My family loves when I make this ham. I'm not sure which they love more, though: eating it straight away or as leftovers on sandwiches.
—Angela Lively, Conroe, TX

PREP: 10 MIN. • **COOK:** 4 HOURS
MAKES: 15 SERVINGS

- 1 spiral-sliced fully cooked bone-in ham (5 lbs.)
- 1 cup unsweetened pineapple juice
- ½ cup packed brown sugar
- ¼ cup butter, melted
- 2 Tbsp. cider vinegar
- 1 garlic clove, minced
- ½ tsp. crushed red pepper flakes
- 1 medium onion, sliced

1. Place ham in a 5-qt. slow cooker. In a small bowl, combine pineapple juice, brown sugar, butter, cider vinegar, garlic and red pepper flakes; pour over ham. Top with onion slices.
2. Cook, covered, on low until a thermometer reads 140°, 4-5 hours. Serve warm.

3 OZ. HAM 194 cal., 7g fat (3g sat. fat), 75mg chol., 821mg sod., 11g carb. (10g sugars, 0 fiber), 22g pro.

NEW ORLEANS-STYLE SPICY SHRIMP

We have family members who attended college in New Orleans. This shrimp captures their favorite flavors from the Big Easy, with the right touches of spice and heat.
—Susan Seymour, Valatie, NY

PREP: 15 MIN. • **BAKE:** 20 MIN. • **MAKES:** 12 SERVINGS

- 3 medium lemons, sliced
- 2/3 cup butter, cubed
- 1/2 cup ketchup
- 1/4 cup Worcestershire sauce
- 2 Tbsp. seafood seasoning
- 2 Tbsp. chili garlic sauce
- 2 Tbsp. Louisiana-style hot sauce
- 1 Tbsp. Italian salad dressing mix
- 4 lbs. uncooked shell-on shrimp (31-40 per lb.)
- 2 bay leaves
- French bread

1. Preheat oven to 350°. In a microwave-safe bowl, combine the first 8 ingredients. Microwave, covered, on high 2-3 minutes or until butter is melted; stir until blended.
2. Divide shrimp and bay leaves between 2 ungreased 13x9-in. baking dishes. Add half of the lemon mixture to each dish; toss to combine.
3. Bake, uncovered, 20-25 minutes or until shrimp turn pink, stirring halfway. Remove bay leaves. Serve with bread.

1 CUP 242 cal., 12g fat (7g sat. fat), 211mg chol., 940mg sod., 7g carb. (4g sugars, 0 fiber), 25g pro.

SEASONED TACO MEAT

I got this recipe from the restaurant where I work. Everyone in town loves the blend of different seasonings, and now the secret is out!
—Denise Mumm, Dixon, IA

PREP: 10 MIN. • **COOK:** 35 MIN.
MAKES: 6½ CUPS

- 3 lbs. ground beef
- 2 large onions, chopped
- 2 cups water
- 5 Tbsp. chili powder
- 2 tsp. salt
- 1 tsp. ground cumin
- ¾ tsp. garlic powder
- ¼ to ½ tsp. crushed red pepper flakes

In a large cast-iron skillet or Dutch oven, cook beef and onion over medium heat until meat is no longer pink, breaking it into crumbles; drain. Add water and seasonings. Bring to a boil. Reduce heat; simmer, uncovered, until the water is evaporated, about 15 minutes.

¼ CUP 113 cal., 7g fat (3g sat. fat), 35mg chol., 277mg sod., 2g carb. (1g sugars, 1g fiber), 10g pro.

PIZZA MACARONI & CHEESE

My grandma made this for us once during a visit, and I never forgot just how good it was. Since my kids love anything with pepperoni and cheese, I bake it so they can enjoy it as much as I did.
—Juli Meyers, Hinesville, GA

PREP: 30 MIN. • **BAKE:** 25 MIN.
MAKES: 12 SERVINGS

- 2 pkg. (14 oz. each) deluxe macaroni and cheese dinner mix
- ½ cup sour cream
- 1 can (14½ oz.) petite diced tomatoes, drained
- 1 can (15 oz.) pizza sauce
- 1 small green pepper, chopped
- 1 small sweet red pepper, chopped
- 2 cups shredded Italian cheese blend
- 2 oz. sliced pepperoni

1. Preheat oven to 350°. Cook macaroni according to package directions for al dente. Drain; return to pan. Stir in contents of cheese packets and sour cream. Transfer to a greased 13x9-in. baking dish.
2. In a small bowl, combine tomatoes and pizza sauce; drop by spoonfuls over macaroni. Top with peppers, cheese and pepperoni. Bake, uncovered, until bubbly, 25-30 minutes.

1 CUP 340 cal., 14g fat (7g sat. fat), 37mg chol., 927mg sod., 37g carb. (5g sugars, 3g fiber), 14g pro.

MEDITERRANEAN COBB SALAD

I'm a huge fan of taking classic dishes and adding some flair to them. I also like to change up heavier dishes, like the classic Cobb salad. I've traded out typical chicken for crunchy falafel that's just as satisfying.
—Jenn Tidwell, Fair Oaks, CA

PREP: 1 HOUR • **COOK:** 5 MIN./BATCH • **MAKES:** 10 SERVINGS

- 1 pkg. (6 oz.) falafel mix
- ½ cup sour cream or plain yogurt
- ¼ cup chopped seeded peeled cucumber
- ¼ cup 2% milk
- 1 tsp. minced fresh parsley
- ¼ tsp. salt
- 4 cups torn romaine
- 4 cups fresh baby spinach
- 3 hard-boiled large eggs, chopped
- 2 medium tomatoes, seeded and finely chopped
- 1 medium ripe avocado, peeled and finely chopped
- ¾ cup crumbled feta cheese
- 8 bacon strips, cooked and crumbled
- ½ cup pitted Greek olives, finely chopped

1. Prepare and cook falafel according to package directions. When cool enough to handle, crumble or coarsely chop falafel.
2. In a small bowl, mix sour cream, cucumber, milk, parsley and salt. In a large bowl, combine romaine and spinach; transfer to a platter. Arrange crumbled falafel and remaining ingredients over greens. Drizzle with dressing.

1 CUP 258 cal., 18g fat (5g sat. fat), 83mg chol., 687mg sod., 15g carb. (3g sugars, 5g fiber), 13g pro.

SMOKED PORK BUTT

Low and slow is the best way to go when cooking pork butt, and it happens perfectly in a smoker. This has very little hands-on time, but you will need to plan for a long cook time. The fantastic thing is the meat freezes very well so you can make it ahead of time and have it ready to go.
—James Schend, Pleasant Prairie, WI

PREP: 10 MIN. + STANDING **SMOKE:** 7 HOURS + RESTING
MAKES: 24 SERVINGS

- 1 bone-in pork shoulder roast (8 to 10 lbs.)
- Applewood chips or pellets
- 3 Tbsp. spicy brown mustard
- ¼ cup All-Purpose Meat Seasoning or favorite spice rub
- ⅓ cup apple cider or juice
- 3 Tbsp. cider vinegar

1. Let roast stand at room temperature for 1 hour. Preheat smoker to 275°. Add wood chips or pellets to smoker according to manufacturer's directions.
2. Trim excess fat from pork, leaving some exterior fat. Pat the roast dry; rub with mustard and sprinkle with spice rub. Place pork in smoker. In a spray bottle, combine apple cider and vinegar; lightly spritz pork. Smoke, spritzing pork every hour, until pork reaches 165° and is a dark brown color, about 5 hours.
3. Transfer pork to a 13x9-in. baking pan or large cast-iron skillet; liberally spritz with cider mixture. Cover tightly with foil and return to smoker. Cook until pork reaches desired degree of doneness. For sliced pork, cook until pork reaches 190° to 195°, 2-3 hours longer. For pulled pork, cook until 200° to 205°. Remove and let rest at room temperature, covered, 45-60 minutes. For slices, cut around bone and cut roast into slices. For pulled pork, remove bone and shred pork. Skim fat from cooking juices; toss pork with cooking juices.

FREEZE OPTION Freeze cooled pork and juices in freezer containers. To use, partially thaw in refrigerator overnight. Heat through in a saucepan, stirring occasionally; add broth or water if necessary.

4 OZ. COOKED PORK 186 cal., 11g fat (4g sat. fat), 67mg chol., 548mg sod., 0 carb. (0 sugars, 0 fiber), 19g pro.

ARTICHOKE SHRIMP PASTA SALAD

I have enjoyed this entree salad as long as I can remember. My mom made it famous, and she passed it down to me on my wedding day. It's one of those potluck staples that folks can't get enough of.
—Mary McCarley, Charlotte, NC

PREP: 20 MIN. • **COOK:** 10 MIN. + CHILLING • **MAKES:** 12 SERVINGS

- 1 pkg. (16 oz.) bow tie pasta
- 2 lbs. peeled and deveined cooked shrimp (16-20 per lb.)
- 2 cans (7½ oz. each) marinated quartered artichoke hearts, drained
- 2 cans (2¼ oz. each) sliced ripe olives, drained
- 2 cups crumbled feta cheese
- 8 green onions, sliced
- ½ cup chopped fresh parsley
- ¼ cup chopped fresh basil

DRESSING

- ½ cup white wine vinegar
- ½ cup olive oil
- ¼ cup lemon juice
- 2 Tbsp. chopped fresh basil
- 2 tsp. Dijon mustard
- Fresh ground pepper, optional

1. Cook pasta according to package directions for al dente. Drain pasta; rinse with cold water and drain well. In a large bowl, combine pasta, shrimp, artichokes, olives, cheese, green onions, parsley and basil.

2. In a small bowl, whisk vinegar, oil, lemon juice, basil, mustard and, if desired, pepper. Pour dressing over pasta mixture; toss to coat. Refrigerate, covered, 2 hours before serving.

1⅓ CUPS 453 cal., 23g fat (7g sat. fat), 135mg chol., 757mg sod., 34g carb. (2g sugars, 6g fiber), 28g pro.

p. 88

Grilled Greats

GRILLED BEER BRATS WITH KRAUT

I made this for my son's 21st birthday bonfire, attended by both friends and family. The kraut flavors are a fabulous topping for this tasty brat.
—Keeley Weber, Sterling Heights, MI

PREP: 45 MIN. • **GRILL:** 35 MIN. • **MAKES:** 12 SERVINGS

- 6 bacon strips, chopped
- 1 large onion, chopped
- 1 medium apple, peeled and thinly sliced
- 2 garlic cloves, minced
- 1 can (14 oz.) sauerkraut, rinsed and well drained
- 3 Tbsp. spicy brown mustard
- 1 Tbsp. brown sugar
- 12 uncooked bratwurst links
- 1 bottle (12 oz.) dark beer
- 12 hoagie buns, split

1. In a large skillet, cook bacon over medium heat until crisp, stirring occasionally. Remove with a slotted spoon; drain on paper towels.
2. Cook and stir onion in bacon drippings until softened. Reduce heat to medium-low; cook 15-20 minutes or until deep golden brown, stirring occasionally. Add apple and garlic; cook 2 minutes longer. Stir in sauerkraut, mustard, brown sugar and cooked bacon.
3. Transfer to a 13x9-in. disposable foil pan. Arrange bratwurst over top. Pour beer over the bratwurst. Place pan on grill rack over medium heat; cook, covered, 30-35 minutes or until sausages are no longer pink. Remove pan from heat.
4. Remove bratwurst from pan and return to grill. Grill, covered, 2-3 minutes on each side or until browned. Serve on buns with sauerkraut mixture.

1 SERVING 582 cal., 34g fat (11g sat. fat), 71mg chol., 1473mg sod., 44g carb. (9g sugars, 2g fiber), 22g pro.

SPICY BARBECUED CHICKEN

This zesty chicken is fantastic served with basil-buttered grilled corn on the cob and fresh coleslaw.
—Rita Wintrode, Corryton, TN

TAKES: 30 MIN. • **MAKES:** 8 SERVINGS

- 1 Tbsp. canola oil
- 2 garlic cloves, minced
- ½ cup chili sauce
- 3 Tbsp. brown sugar
- 2 tsp. salt-free seasoning blend, divided
- ¾ tsp. cayenne pepper, divided
- 2 tsp. ground mustard
- 2 tsp. chili powder
- 8 boneless skinless chicken breast halves (4 oz. each)

1. In a small saucepan, heat oil over medium heat. Add garlic; cook and stir 1 minute. Add chili sauce, brown sugar, 1 tsp. seasoning blend and ¼ tsp. cayenne. Bring to a boil; cook and stir for 1 minute. Remove from the heat.
2. In a small bowl, mix mustard, chili powder and the remaining seasoning blend and cayenne; rub over chicken.
3. On a lightly oiled grill rack, grill the chicken, covered, over medium heat for 4 minutes. Turn; grill for 4-6 minutes longer or until a thermometer reads 165°, brushing tops occasionally with the chili sauce mixture.

1 CHICKEN BREAST HALF 179 cal., 5g fat (1g sat. fat), 63mg chol., 293mg sod., 10g carb. (8g sugars, 0 fiber), 23g pro.

BRATWURST SUPPER

This simple dinner grills to perfection in heavy-duty foil packets. Loaded with chunks of bratwurst, red potatoes, mushrooms and carrots, it's easy to season with onion soup mix and a little soy sauce.
—Janice Meyer, Medford, WI

PREP: 10 MIN. • **GRILL:** 50 MIN. • **MAKES:** 12 SERVINGS

- 3 lbs. uncooked bratwurst links
- 3 lbs. small red potatoes, cut into wedges
- 1 lb. baby carrots
- 1 large red onion, sliced and separated into rings
- 8 oz. whole fresh mushrooms
- ¼ cup butter, cubed
- 1 envelope onion soup mix
- 2 Tbsp. soy sauce
- ½ tsp. pepper

1. For each of 2 foil packets, arrange a double thickness of heavy-duty foil (about 17x15 in.) on a flat surface.
2. Cut brats into thirds. Divide the brats, potatoes, carrots, onion and mushrooms evenly between the 2 double-layer foil rectangles. Dot with butter. Sprinkle with soup mix, soy sauce and pepper. Bring the edges of foil together; crimp to seal, forming 2 large packets. Seal tightly; turn to coat.
3. Grill, covered, over medium heat for 23-28 minutes on each side or until vegetables are tender and sausage is no longer pink. Open foil carefully to allow steam to escape.

1 SERVING 524 cal., 37g fat (14g sat. fat), 94mg chol., 1445mg sod., 28g carb. (4g sugars, 3g fiber), 19g pro.

SPICE-RUBBED RIBS

For grilling, here's the rub I recommend. If you have some left after making ribs, put it in a shaker and use it another day on pork or beef roasts, tenderloins, steaks and more. It's also amazing alone or under sauce.
—Cheryl Ewing, Ellwood City, PA

PREP: 10 MIN. • **GRILL:** 1 HOUR
MAKES: 10 SERVINGS

- 3 Tbsp. paprika
- 2 Tbsp. plus 1 tsp. salt
- 2 Tbsp. plus 1 tsp. garlic powder
- 2 Tbsp. cayenne pepper
- 4 tsp. onion powder
- 4 tsp. dried oregano
- 4 tsp. dried thyme
- 4 tsp. pepper
- 10 lbs. pork baby back ribs

1. In a small bowl, combine the seasonings; rub over ribs.
2. Prepare grill for indirect heat, using a drip pan. Grill the ribs, covered, over indirect medium heat for 1 hour or until meat is tender, turning occasionally.

1 LB. 792 cal., 62g fat (23g sat. fat), 245mg chol., 1864mg sod., 5g carb. (0 sugars, 2g fiber), 51g pro.

GLAZED SPATCHCOCKED CHICKEN

A few pantry items, such as mustard and apricot preserves, inspired this recipe. And since then it has been the successful centerpiece for both weeknight meals and big parties alike.
—James Schend, Pleasant Prairie, WI

PREP: 15 MIN. • **GRILL:** 40 MINUTES + STANDING • **MAKES:** 6 SERVINGS

- **1 cup white wine or chicken broth**
- **1 cup apricot preserves or quince jelly**
- **1 Tbsp. stone-ground mustard**
- **1 broiler/fryer chicken (3 to 4 lbs.)**
- **¾ tsp. salt**
- **½ tsp. pepper**

1. In a small saucepan, bring wine to a boil; cook 3-4 minutes or until wine is reduced by half. Stir in the preserves and mustard. Reserve half the glaze for basting.
2. Cut the chicken along each side of the backbone with shears. Remove the backbone. Turn the chicken breast side up, and press to flatten. Sprinkle with salt and pepper.
3. Prepare grill for indirect medium heat. Place chicken on greased grill grate, skin side down, covered, over direct heat until nicely browned, 10-15 minutes. Turn the chicken and place over indirect heat until a thermometer in the thickest part of the thigh reads 170°-175°, brushing occasionally with reserved glaze mixture, about 30 minutes.
4. Remove chicken from grill. Let stand 15 minutes before carving; serve with remaining glaze.

5 OZ. COOKED CHICKEN 437 cal., 17g fat (5g sat. fat), 104mg chol., 458mg sod., 35g carb. (23g sugars, 0 fiber), 34g pro.

SPIEDIS

This is our favorite cookout dish. The recipe originated here in my hometown in the 1930s. Our meat preference for this recipe is venison, but we use others when it's not available.
—Gertrude Skinner, Binghamton, NY

PREP: 10 MIN. + MARINATING
GRILL: 10 MIN.
MAKES: 8 SERVINGS

- 1 cup canola oil
- 2/3 cup cider vinegar
- 2 Tbsp. Worcestershire sauce
- 1/2 medium onion, finely chopped
- 1/2 tsp. salt
- 1/2 tsp. sugar
- 1/2 tsp. dried basil
- 1/2 tsp. dried marjoram
- 1/2 tsp. dried rosemary, crushed
- 2 1/2 lbs. boneless lean pork, beef, lamb, venison, chicken or turkey, cut into 1 1/2- to 2-in. cubes
- Italian rolls or hot dog buns

1. In a glass or plastic bowl, combine the first 9 ingredients. Add meat and toss to coat. Cover and refrigerate for 24 hours, stirring occasionally.
2. Drain meat, discarding marinade. Thread meat onto metal or soaked wooden skewers. Grill, covered, over medium heat 10-15 minutes or until the meat reaches desired doneness, turning occasionally. Remove meat from skewers and serve on long Italian rolls or hot dog buns.

4 OZ. COOKED MEAT 205 cal., 12g fat (0 sat. fat), 42mg chol., 104mg sod., 1g carb. (0 sugars, 0 fiber), 22g pro.

JERSEY-STYLE HOT DOGS

I grew up in northern New Jersey, where this way of eating hot dogs—with cooked potatoes, peppers and onions—was created. My husband never had them as a kid but has come to love them even more than I do. The combination of ingredients and flavors is simple, but just right!
—Suzanne Banfield, Basking Ridge, NJ

PREP: 20 MIN. • **GRILL:** 40 MIN.
MAKES: 12 SERVINGS (10 CUPS POTATO MIXTURE)

- **6 medium Yukon Gold potatoes (about 3 lbs.), halved and thinly sliced**
- **3 large sweet red peppers, thinly sliced**
- **3 large onions, halved and thinly sliced**
- **⅓ cup olive oil**
- **6 garlic cloves, minced**
- **3 tsp. salt**
- **1½ tsp. pepper**
- **12 bun-length beef hot dogs**
- **12 hot dog buns, split**

1. In a large bowl, combine the potatoes, red peppers and onions. In a small bowl, mix oil, garlic, salt and pepper; add to potato mixture and toss to coat.
2. Transfer to two 13x9-in. disposable foil pans; cover with foil. Place pans on grill rack over medium heat; cook, covered, for 30-35 minutes or until potatoes are tender. Remove from heat.
3. Grill hot dogs, covered, over medium heat 7-9 minutes or until heated through, turning occasionally. Place buns on grill, cut side down; grill until lightly toasted. Place hot dogs and potato mixture in buns. Serve with remaining potato mixture.

1 SERVING 453 cal., 24g fat (8g sat. fat), 35mg chol., 1261mg sod., 48g carb. (8g sugars, 4g fiber), 13g pro.

EASY GRILLED JERK CHICKEN

This easy grilled jerk chicken uses a Scotch bonnet pepper for extra heat and an impressive homemade seasoning blend. If you keep your spice cabinet well stocked, you probably have most of these ingredients on hand.
—Cathy Trochelman, Brookfield, WI

PREP: 20 MIN. + MARINATING • **GRILL:** 30 MIN. • **MAKES:** 8 SERVINGS

- 1 Scotch bonnet pepper, seeds and ribs removed, finely minced
- 6 garlic cloves, minced
- 4 Tbsp. reduced-sodium soy sauce
- 4 Tbsp. packed brown sugar
- 4 tsp. paprika
- 4 tsp. ground ginger
- 4 tsp. ground allspice
- 3 tsp. salt
- 2 tsp. onion powder
- 1 tsp. pepper
- 1 tsp. dried thyme
- ½ tsp. ground cinnamon
- ½ tsp. ground nutmeg
- ½ tsp. cayenne pepper
- 8 bone-in, skin-on chicken thighs (about 3 lbs.)
- Hot sauce, optional

1. In a large glass bowl, combine first 14 ingredients. Add chicken; toss to coat. Cover; refrigerate at least 1 hour or overnight.

2. Preheat grill to medium. Grill the chicken, covered, over indirect medium heat for 30-40 minutes or until a thermometer reaches 170°-175°. If desired, serve with hot sauce.

6 OZ. COOKED CHICKEN 272 cal., 15g fat (4g sat. fat), 81mg chol., 1245mg sod., 11g carb. (7g sugars, 1g fiber), 24g pro.

MEXICAN STREET CORN

Elote, otherwise known as Mexican street corn, is grilled, covered in mayo, and then sprinkled with chili powder, Cotija and cilantro. A squeeze of lime juice is the perfect finishing touch.
—James Schend, Pleasant Prairie, WI

PREP: 15 MIN. + SOAKING
GRILL: 25 MIN.
MAKES: 6 SERVINGS

- 6 medium ears sweet corn
- ¼ cup sour cream
- ¼ cup mayonnaise
- ¼ cup minced fresh cilantro
- 2 garlic cloves, minced
- 1 tsp. grated lime zest
- 2 Tbsp. lime juice
- 6 Tbsp. Cotija cheese
- 2 to 3 tsp. chili powder

1. Carefully peel back corn husks to within 1 in. of bottoms; remove silk. Rewrap corn in husks; secure with butcher's twine. Place in a Dutch oven; cover with cold water. Soak 20 minutes; drain.
2. Grill corn, covered, over medium heat 25-30 minutes or until tender, turning often.
3. Meanwhile, in a small bowl, combine sour cream, mayonnaise, cilantro, garlic, lime zest and lime juice. Peel back husks; spread sour cream mixture over corn. Sprinkle with Cotija cheese and chili powder. Serve immediately.

1 EAR 278 cal., 22g fat (4g sat. fat), 14mg chol., 245mg sod., 20g carb. (6g sugars, 2g fiber), 5g pro.

BURGERS WITH SPICY DILL SALSA

When I make burgers or hot dogs for barbecues, I also make a must-try topping. Pile it on anything!
—Valonda Seward, Coarsegold, CA

PREP: 20 MIN.
GRILL: 10 MIN./BATCH
MAKES: 12 SERVINGS (3 CUPS SALSA)

- 1 jar (10 oz.) dill pickle relish
- 3 plum tomatoes, seeded and finely chopped
- 1 small white onion, finely chopped
- ½ cup finely chopped red onion
- ½ cup minced fresh cilantro
- 1 Tbsp. olive oil
- 1 to 2 serrano peppers, seeded and chopped

BURGERS

- 3 lbs. ground beef
- 2 tsp. salt
- 1 tsp. pepper
- 12 hamburger buns, split

1. In a bowl, mix first 7 ingredients. In another bowl, combine beef, salt and pepper; mix lightly but thoroughly. Shape into twelve ½-in.-thick patties.
2. In 2 batches, grill the burgers, covered, over medium heat or broil 4 in. from heat 4-5 minutes on each side or until a thermometer reads 160°. Serve with salsa.

NOTE Wear disposable gloves when cutting hot peppers; the oils can burn skin. Avoid touching your face.

1 BURGER WITH ¼ CUP SALSA 371 cal., 16g fat (6g sat. fat), 70mg chol., 926mg sod., 31g carb. (4g sugars, 2g fiber), 25g pro.

STEAK & SHRIMP KABOBS

You'll make any get-together special with these attractive kabobs. Cubes of marinated steak are skewered with shrimp, mushrooms, tomatoes, green peppers and onions, then grilled. For picnics, I assemble the kabobs at home and carry them in a large container.
—Karen Mergener, St. Croix, MN

PREP: 20 MIN. + MARINATING • **GRILL:** 15 MIN. • **MAKES:** 8 SERVINGS

- 1 cup teriyaki sauce
- 1 can (6 oz.) pineapple juice
- ½ cup packed brown sugar
- 6 garlic cloves, minced
- ¼ tsp. Worcestershire sauce
- ⅛ tsp. pepper
- 1 lb. beef top sirloin steak, cut into 1-in. cubes
- 1 lb. uncooked shrimp (26-30 per lb.), peeled and deveined
- 1 lb. whole fresh mushrooms
- 2 large green peppers, cut into 1-in. pieces
- 2 medium onions, halved and quartered
- 1 pint cherry tomatoes
- 1½ tsp. cornstarch

1. In a large bowl, combine the first 6 ingredients. Pour half the marinade into a shallow dish; add beef. Cover and refrigerate 8 hours or overnight, turning occasionally. Cover and refrigerate remaining marinade.
2. Drain beef, discarding marinade. On metal or soaked wooden skewers, alternately thread the beef, shrimp, mushrooms, green peppers, onions and tomatoes. In a small saucepan, combine the cornstarch and reserved marinade until smooth. Bring to a boil; cook and stir until thickened, 1-2 minutes.
3. Prepare grill for indirect heat, using a drip pan. Place kabobs over drip pan and grill, covered, over indirect medium heat for 5 minutes. Turn and brush with thickened marinade. Cover and cook until shrimp turn pink and beef reaches desired doneness, 5-10 minutes, turning and brushing occasionally.

1 KABOB 258 cal., 3g fat (1g sat. fat), 92mg chol., 1326mg sod., 30g carb. (24g sugars, 2g fiber), 26g pro.

MIX IT UP

What are some variations of these steak and shrimp kabobs? It's easy to swap in different ingredients for kabobs, as long as they hold up well on the grill. Try using zucchini, asparagus, yellow squash or even pineapple. You can also replace the sirloin with ribeye or New York strip steak.

GINGER SALMON WITH CUCUMBER LIME SAUCE

Lime with ginger is a favorite flavor combo for me, especially with grilled salmon. So good! Even with the cucumber sauce, this recipe is easy too.
—*Noelle Myers, Grand Forks, ND*

PREP: 30 MIN. • **GRILL:** 10 MIN. • **MAKES:** 10 SERVINGS

- 1 Tbsp. grated lime zest
- ¼ cup lime juice
- 2 Tbsp. olive oil
- 2 Tbsp. rice vinegar or white wine vinegar
- 4 tsp. sugar
- ½ tsp. salt
- ½ tsp. ground coriander
- ½ tsp. freshly ground pepper
- ⅓ cup chopped fresh cilantro
- 1 Tbsp. finely chopped onion
- 2 tsp. minced fresh gingerroot
- 2 garlic cloves, minced
- 2 medium cucumbers, peeled, seeded and chopped

SALMON

- ⅓ cup minced fresh gingerroot
- 1 Tbsp. lime juice
- 1 Tbsp. olive oil
- ½ tsp. salt
- ½ tsp. freshly ground pepper
- 10 salmon fillets (6 oz. each)

1. Place the first 13 ingredients in a blender. Cover and process until pureed.
2. In a small bowl, mix ginger, lime juice, oil, salt and pepper. Rub over flesh side of salmon fillets.
3. Place salmon on a lightly oiled grill rack, skin side down. Grill, covered, over medium-high heat 10-12 minutes or until fish just begins to flake easily with a fork. Serve with sauce.

1 SERVING 327 cal., 20g fat (4g sat. fat), 85mg chol., 372mg sod., 7g carb. (4g sugars, 1g fiber), 29g pro.

Reader Review

"I made this last night, and I thought I'd died and gone to heaven. The tastes were fantastic. Love, love, love this! Will definitely be making again soon!"
—MELISSA_IN_NJ, TASTEOFHOME.COM

STEAK WITH CHIPOTLE-LIME CHIMICHURRI

Steak gets a flavor kick from chimichurri. This piquant, all-purpose herb sauce is so versatile, it complements most any grilled meat, poultry or fish.
—Laureen Pittman, Riverside, CA

TAKES: 30 MIN. • **MAKES:** 8 SERVINGS

- **2 cups fresh parsley leaves**
- **1½ cups fresh cilantro leaves**
- **½ medium red onion, coarsely chopped**
- **1 to 2 chipotle peppers in adobo sauce**
- **5 garlic cloves, sliced**
- **½ cup olive oil**
- **¼ cup white wine vinegar**
- **1 tsp. grated lime zest**
- **¼ cup lime juice**
- **3 tsp. dried oregano**
- **1¼ tsp. salt, divided**
- **¾ tsp. pepper, divided**
- **2 lbs. beef flat iron steaks or 2 beef top sirloin steaks (1 lb. each)**

1. For chimichurri, place the first 5 ingredients in a food processor; pulse until finely chopped. Add oil, vinegar, lime zest, lime juice, oregano, ½ tsp. salt and ¼ tsp. pepper; process until blended. Transfer to a bowl; refrigerate, covered, until serving.
2. Sprinkle the steaks with the remaining salt and pepper. Grill, covered, over medium heat for 5-8 minutes on each side or until meat reaches desired doneness (for medium-rare, a thermometer should read 135°; medium, 140°; medium-well, 145°). Let stand 5 minutes before slicing. Serve with chimichurri.

3 OZ. COOKED STEAK WITH 3 TBSP. SAUCE 336 cal., 26g fat (7g sat. fat), 73mg chol., 462mg sod., 4g carb. (1g sugars, 1g fiber), 22g pro.

DILLY BARBECUED TURKEY

This is one of my brother-in-law's special cookout recipes. The onions, garlic and herbs in the marinade make a tasty, tender turkey, and the tempting aroma prompts the family to gather around the grill.
—Sue Walker, Greentown, IN

PREP: 10 MIN. + MARINATING
GRILL: 50 MIN. + STANDING
MAKES: 12 SERVINGS

- 1 cup plain yogurt
- ½ cup lemon juice
- ⅓ cup canola oil
- ½ cup minced fresh parsley
- ½ cup chopped green onions
- 4 garlic cloves, minced
- 4 Tbsp. fresh minced dill or 4 tsp. dill weed
- 1 tsp. dried rosemary, crushed
- 1 tsp. salt
- ½ tsp. pepper
- 2 bone-in turkey breast halves (2½ to 3 lbs. each)

1. In a large bowl, combine the first 10 ingredients. Pour half of mixture into a shallow dish. Add turkey and turn to coat. Cover and refrigerate 6-8 hours or overnight. Cover and refrigerate remaining marinade.
2. Drain the turkey, discarding marinade. Grill turkey, covered, over medium-hot heat, basting occasionally with the reserved marinade, 50-65 minutes or until a thermometer reads 170°. Let stand 10 minutes before slicing.

4 OZ. COOKED TURKEY 198 cal., 4g fat (1g sat. fat), 98mg chol., 271mg sod., 2g carb. (1g sugars, 0 fiber), 36g pro.

GRILLED DIJON PORK ROAST

I came up with this recipe one day after not having much in the house to eat. My husband loved it, and it has become the only way I make pork now.
—Cyndi Lacy-Andersen, Woodinville, WA

PREP: 10 MIN. + MARINATING
GRILL: 1 HOUR + STANDING
MAKES: 12 SERVINGS

- ⅓ cup balsamic vinegar
- 3 Tbsp. Dijon mustard
- 1 Tbsp. honey
- 1 tsp. salt
- 1 boneless pork loin roast (3 to 4 lbs.)

1. In a bowl or shallow dish, whisk vinegar, mustard, honey and salt. Add pork; turn to coat. Cover and refrigerate at least 8 hours or overnight.
2. Prepare grill for indirect heat, using a drip pan.
3. Drain pork, discarding marinade. Place pork on a greased grill rack over drip pan and cook, covered, over indirect medium heat for 1-1½ hours or until a thermometer reads 145°, turning occasionally. Let stand 10 minutes before slicing.

3 OZ. COOKED PORK 149 cal., 5g fat (2g sat. fat), 56mg chol., 213mg sod., 2g carb. (1g sugars, 0 fiber), 22g pro.

KANSAS CITY-STYLE RIBS

Our family recipe for ribs has evolved over the years to near perfection. These country-style beauties are legendary in our close circle.
—Linda Schend, Kenosha, WI

PREP: 10 MIN. + CHILLING • **GRILL:** 1 HOUR 25 MIN. • **MAKES:** 12 SERVINGS

- 1⅓ cups packed brown sugar
- 2 tsp. each garlic powder, onion powder and smoked paprika
- 1¼ tsp. each ground cumin, coarsely ground pepper and cayenne pepper
- 12 bone-in country-style pork ribs (about 7 lbs.)

SAUCE

- 2 Tbsp. canola oil
- 1 medium onion, finely chopped
- 1 cup tomato sauce
- ⅓ cup dark brown sugar
- ¼ cup ketchup
- ¼ cup molasses
- 1 Tbsp. apple cider vinegar
- 2 tsp. Worcestershire sauce
- 1 tsp. salt
- 1 tsp. ground mustard
- ¼ tsp. smoked paprika
- ¼ tsp. cayenne pepper

1. In a small bowl, mix brown sugar and seasonings; sprinkle over ribs. Refrigerate, covered, at least 1 hour.
2. For sauce, in a large saucepan, heat oil over medium heat. Add onion; cook and stir until tender, 5-6 minutes. Stir in remaining ingredients; bring to a boil, stirring occasionally. Remove from heat.
3. Wrap ribs in a large piece of heavy-duty foil; seal edges of foil. Grill the ribs, covered, over indirect medium heat until ribs are tender, 1¼-¾ hours.
4. Carefully remove ribs from foil. Place the ribs over direct medium heat; baste with some of the sauce. Grill, covered, 8-10 minutes or until browned, turning and basting occasionally with remaining sauce.

1 RIB 453 cal., 18g fat (6g sat. fat), 101mg chol., 452mg sod., 40g carb. (36g sugars, 1g fiber), 31g pro.

PILE ON THE FLAVOR

This dry rub is great on chicken and pork chops, too, so make a big batch of it. Keep it in a canister in your cabinet for spur-of-the-moment grilling.

GRILLED LIME CHICKEN

My family is always delighted when I tell them these grilled chicken breasts are on the menu. Everyone loves the wonderful marinade; I relish the ease of preparation.
—Lisa Dougherty, Vacaville, CA

PREP: 10 MIN. + MARINATING
GRILL: 10 MIN.
MAKES: 8 SERVINGS

- 8 boneless skinless chicken breast halves (4 oz. each)
- ½ cup lime juice
- ⅓ cup olive oil
- 4 green onions, chopped
- 4 garlic cloves, minced
- 3 Tbsp. chopped fresh dill, divided
- ¼ tsp. pepper
- Lime wedges, optional

1. Place chicken in a shallow dish. Combine the lime juice, oil, onions, garlic, 2 Tbsp. dill and pepper; pour over the chicken and turn to coat. Refrigerate, covered, 2-4 hours.
2. Drain the chicken, discarding marinade. Grill chicken, covered, over medium-hot heat for 3-4 minutes on each side or until a thermometer reads 165°. Sprinkle with remaining 1 Tbsp. dill. Serve with lime wedges if desired.

1 CHICKEN BREAST HALF 127 cal., 3g fat (1g sat. fat), 63mg chol., 56mg sod., 1g carb. (0 sugars, 0 fiber), 23g pro.

GRILLED VEGGIES WITH CAPER BUTTER

We enjoy the tart, peppery taste of capers. No one likes a bland veggie, and caper butter helps peppers, squash and zucchini shine.
—*Danyelle Crum, Indian Trail, NC*

PREP: 25 MIN. • **GRILL:** 10 MIN. • **MAKES:** 8 SERVINGS

- ¼ cup butter, cubed
- 2 garlic cloves, minced
- 1 Tbsp. lemon juice
- 2 tsp. capers, drained and chopped
- 1 Tbsp. minced fresh parsley
- 2 medium zucchini, cut in half lengthwise
- 2 medium crookneck or yellow summer squash, cut in half lengthwise
- 1 medium sweet yellow or orange pepper, quartered
- 1 medium sweet red pepper, quartered
- 2 large portobello mushrooms, stems removed
- 3 green onions, trimmed
- 2 Tbsp. olive oil
- ½ tsp. salt
- ¼ tsp. pepper

1. In a small saucepan, melt butter over medium-low heat. Add garlic; cook 2 minutes. Add lemon juice and capers; cook 2 minutes. Stir in parsley.
2. Brush vegetables with oil; sprinkle with salt and pepper.
3. Grill zucchini, squash and peppers, covered, over medium heat 4-5 minutes on each side or until crisp-tender, basting occasionally with butter mixture. Grill the mushrooms and onions, covered, 1-2 minutes on each side or until tender, basting occasionally with butter mixture.
4. Cut the vegetables as desired; transfer to a serving platter. Drizzle with remaining butter mixture.

1 SERVING 117 cal., 10g fat (4g sat. fat), 15mg chol., 219mg sod., 7g carb. (3g sugars, 2g fiber), 2g pro.

p. 112

Sweet Treats

LEMON BLUEBERRY TART

When it's blueberry season, you have to try this amazing combination of flavors. Lemon adds a zesty counterpoint to the tart's fruit topping and buttery crust.
—Erin Chilcoat, Central Islip, NY

PREP: 40 MIN. + CHILLING • **BAKE:** 15 MIN. + CHILLING
MAKES: 12 SERVINGS

- 1¼ cups all-purpose flour
- ⅓ cup sugar
- ¼ tsp. salt
- ½ cup cold butter, cubed
- 1 large egg yolk
- 2 Tbsp. cold water
- 1 tsp. vanilla extract

FILLING

- 1 can (14 oz.) sweetened condensed milk
- ½ cup lemon juice
- 4 large egg yolks
- 4 tsp. grated lemon zest
- Dash salt

TOPPING

- 2 cups fresh blueberries
- ½ cup blueberry spreadable fruit

1. In a large bowl, combine the flour, sugar and salt; cut in butter until mixture resembles coarse crumbs. Whisk egg yolk, water and vanilla; add to crumb mixture. Stir until dough forms a ball. Cover and refrigerate at least 30 minutes.
2. On a floured surface, roll dough into an 11-in. circle. Transfer to a greased 9-in. fluted tart pan with a removable bottom; trim even with edge of pan. Place pan on a baking sheet.
3. Line the unpricked crust with a double thickness of heavy-duty foil. Bake at 375° for 15 minutes. Remove foil; bake 5 minutes longer.
4. In a small bowl, beat the filling ingredients; pour into crust. Bake for 12-15 minutes or until set. Cool on a wire rack.
5. For topping, microwave fresh blueberries and spreadable fruit on high for 1-2 minutes or until bubbly around the edges; stir. Cool for 5-10 minutes. Gently spoon over filling. Refrigerate until chilled.

1 PIECE 308 cal., 12g fat (7g sat. fat), 117mg chol., 161mg sod., 45g carb. (32g sugars, 1g fiber), 5g pro.

COPYCAT CHEESECAKE FACTORY ORIGINAL CHEESECAKE

If you're going to prepare cheesecake, why not re-create one of the most popular desserts in the country? It's easier than you think when you follow this four-step recipe.
—Taste of Home *Test Kitchen*

PREP: 30 MIN. + COOLING • **BAKE:** 1½ HOURS + CHILLING • **MAKES:** 16 SERVINGS

- 2½ cups graham cracker crumbs
- ¼ cup sugar
- ½ cup butter, melted

FILLING

- 4 pkg. (8 oz. each) cream cheese, softened
- 2 cups sour cream
- 1¾ cups sugar
- 1 Tbsp. vanilla extract
- 4 large eggs, room temperature, lightly beaten

TOPPING

- 1 cup sour cream
- ¼ cup sugar

1. Preheat oven to 325°. In a small bowl, combine graham cracker crumbs and sugar; stir in butter. Press onto the bottom and up the side of a greased 9-in. springform pan. Place on a baking sheet. Bake until lightly browned, 18-22 minutes. Cool on a wire rack.
2. In a large bowl, beat the cream cheese, sour cream, sugar and vanilla until smooth. Add eggs; beat on low speed just until combined. Pour into crust. Place the pan on a double thickness of heavy-duty foil (about 18-in. square). Securely wrap foil around pan.
3. Place in a larger baking pan; add 1 in. hot water to larger pan. Bake until the center is just set and the top appears dull, about 1½ hours. Remove springform pan from the water bath. Let stand 5 minutes on a wire rack.
4. For topping, in a small bowl, mix sour cream and sugar; spread over top of cheesecake. Bake 5 minutes longer without water bath. Cool for 10 minutes on wire rack. Loosen side from pan with a knife; remove foil. Cool 1 hour longer. Refrigerate cheesecake overnight, covering when completely cooled. Remove rim from pan.

1 PIECE 536 cal., 37g fat (21g sat. fat), 151mg chol., 329mg sod., 45g carb. (36g sugars, 1g fiber), 8g pro.

PATCHWORK QUILT CAKE

This cake has a lovely homemade flavor and tender crumb. Be sure to pile on the buttery frosting, which adds a burst of vanilla.
—Aria Thornton, Milwaukee, WI

PREP: 55 MIN. • **BAKE:** 40 MIN. + COOLING • **MAKES:** 15 SERVINGS

- ⅔ cup butter, softened
- 1¾ cups sugar
- 1 Tbsp. vanilla extract
- 2 large eggs, room temperature
- 2½ cups all-purpose flour
- 2½ tsp. baking powder
- ½ tsp. salt
- 1¼ cups 2% milk

FROSTING

- 1 cup butter, softened
- 3 cups confectioners' sugar
- 4 tsp. vanilla extract
- 3 to 4 Tbsp. heavy whipping cream
- Assorted fresh berries

1. Preheat oven to 350°. Grease a 13x9-in. baking dish.
2. Cream the butter and sugar until light and fluffy, 5-7 minutes. Add the vanilla and eggs, 1 at at time, beating well. In another bowl, whisk together flour, baking powder and salt; beat into creamed mixture alternately with milk. Transfer to prepared dish.
3. Bake 40-45 minutes or until a toothpick inserted in center comes out clean. Place on a wire rack; cool completely.
4. For the frosting, beat the butter until creamy; gradually beat in confectioners' sugar until smooth and light in color, about 3 minutes. Beat in the vanilla and 3 Tbsp. cream until light and fluffy, about 2 minutes; thin with additional cream if desired. Spread over cake. Before serving, top with berries in a patchwork quilt pattern.

1 PIECE 477 cal., 23g fat (14g sat. fat), 84mg chol., 342mg sod., 65g carb. (48g sugars, 1g fiber), 4g pro.

RAINBOW S'MOREO COOKIES

Homemade Oreo-style cookies are pretty great on their own, but they're even better when you add graham cracker crumbs to the cookie dough, stuff them with marshmallow creme and roll them in sprinkles. You can change the color of the sprinkles depending on the holiday or occasion.
—Colleen Delawder, Herndon, VA

PREP: 15 MIN. + CHILLING • **BAKE:** 10 MIN./BATCH + COOLING • **MAKES:** ABOUT 2 DOZEN

- ½ cup unsalted butter, softened
- 1 cup sugar
- 1 large egg, room temperature
- 1 tsp. vanilla extract
- ½ cup baking cocoa
- ¾ cup graham cracker crumbs
- ¾ cup all-purpose flour
- 1 tsp. baking powder
- ¼ tsp. kosher salt
- 1 jar (7 oz.) marshmallow creme
- Rainbow sprinkles

1. Preheat oven to 350°. Cream butter and sugar until light and fluffy, 5-7 minutes. Beat in egg and vanilla. Beat in cocoa. In another bowl, whisk cracker crumbs, flour, baking powder and salt; gradually beat into the creamed mixture. Refrigerate until firm, at least 30 minutes.
2. Shape dough into 1-in. balls. Place 2 in. apart on parchment-lined baking sheets. Flatten with bottom of a glass dipped in sugar. Bake until set, 6-8 minutes. Cool on pans 3 minutes. Remove to wire racks to cool completely.
3. Spread marshmallow creme on bottoms of half of the cookies; cover with remaining cookies. Roll edges in sprinkles. Serve immediately, or freeze the cookies in freezer containers, separating layers with waxed paper. To use, thaw cookies briefly before serving.

1 SANDWICH COOKIE 131 cal., 5g fat (3g sat. fat), 18mg chol., 64mg sod., 20g carb. (14g sugars, 1g fiber), 1g pro.

EASY FOUR-LAYER CHOCOLATE DESSERT

I grew up on this nutty, chocolaty layered treat. Now I make it for both my mom and myself, since I know she loves it too.
—Kristen Stecklein, Waukesha, WI

PREP: 20 MIN. • **BAKE:** 15 MIN. + CHILLING • **MAKES:** 15 SERVINGS

- 1 cup all-purpose flour
- ½ cup cold butter
- 1 cup chopped walnuts, toasted, divided
- 1 pkg. (8 oz.) cream cheese, softened
- 1 cup confectioners' sugar
- 2 cartons (8 oz. each) frozen whipped topping, thawed, divided
- 2½ cups 2% milk
- 2 pkg. (3.9 oz. each) instant chocolate pudding mix
- 1 cup semisweet chocolate chunks
- Chocolate syrup

1. Preheat oven to 350°. Place flour in a small bowl; cut in butter until crumbly. Stir in ½ cup walnuts. Press onto bottom of an ungreased 13x9-in. baking dish. Bake until light golden brown, 12-15 minutes. Cool completely on a wire rack.
2. In a small bowl, beat cream cheese and confectioners' sugar until smooth; fold in 1 carton whipped topping. Spread over crust. In a large bowl, whisk milk and pudding mix for 2 minutes. Gently spread over cream cheese layer. Top with remaining whipped topping. Sprinkle with chocolate chunks and remaining walnuts. Refrigerate until cold.
3. Cut into bars. Just before serving, drizzle with chocolate syrup.

NOTE To toast nuts, bake in a shallow pan in a 350°; oven for 5-10 minutes or cook in a skillet over low heat until lightly browned, stirring occasionally.

1 PIECE 434 cal., 26g fat (15g sat. fat), 36mg chol., 195mg sod., 46g carb. (27g sugars, 2g fiber), 5g pro.

Reader Review

"This recipe is quick and easy and quite delicious. I drizzled caramel topping on top and sprinkled on chocolate chips and leftover chopped toasted walnuts. The baked crust is perfect and tastes delicious with the creamy filling."

—BICKTASW, TASTEOFHOME.COM

SUMMERTIME FUN COOKIES

Use this basic sugar cookie recipe to make the perfect poolside treat. Kids (and adults) won't be able to get enough.
—Coleen Walter, Bancroft, MI

PREP: 30 MIN. • **BAKE:** 10 MIN./BATCH + COOLING
MAKES: ABOUT 2½ DOZEN

- 1 cup butter, softened
- ¾ cup sugar
- 1 tsp. vanilla extract
- ½ tsp. almond extract
- 2 large eggs, room temperature
- 2¼ cups all-purpose flour
- 1 tsp. cream of tartar
- ½ tsp. baking soda
- ¼ tsp. salt
- ¼ tsp. ground nutmeg

FROSTING

- ¼ cup butter, softened
- 3 cups confectioners' sugar
- 1 tsp. almond extract
- 2 to 4 Tbsp. hot water
- Blue food coloring
- Optional decorations: Bear-shaped crackers, fish-shaped graham crackers, Airheads candies, gummy sour rings, white sugar pearls and palm tree party picks

1. Preheat oven to 350°. Cream butter and sugar until light and fluffy, 5-7 minutes; beat in extracts and egg, 1 at a time. In another bowl, whisk together the flour, cream of tartar, baking soda, salt and nutmeg; gradually beat into creamed mixture.
2. Drop the dough by rounded tablespoonfuls 3 in. apart onto parchment-lined baking sheets; flatten slightly with bottom of a glass dipped in sugar. Bake until edges begin to brown, 8-10 minutes. Remove from pan to wire racks; cool completely.
3. For the frosting, beat butter, confectioners' sugar, extract and enough water to reach desired consistency; tint blue with food coloring. Spread over cookies. Decorate as desired.

1 COOKIE 174 cal., 8g fat (5g sat. fat), 33mg chol., 107mg sod., 24g carb. (17g sugars, 0 fiber), 1g pro.

SECRET INGREDIENT

Cream of tartar is an acid. When combined with baking soda, it creates carbon dioxide, helping these cookies puff up just a bit. It also gives them their signature soft texture.

BERRY DREAM CAKE

I use cherry gelatin to give a boxed cake mix an eye-appealing marbled effect. It's so festive-looking. Top it with whatever fruit you like!
—*Margaret McNeil, Germantown, TN*

PREP: 15 MIN. + CHILLING
BAKE: 30 MIN. + CHILLING
MAKES: 15 SERVINGS

- 1 pkg. white cake mix (regular size)
- 1½ cups boiling water
- 1 pkg. (3 oz.) cherry gelatin
- 1 pkg. (8 oz.) cream cheese, softened
- 2 cups whipped topping
- 4 cups fresh strawberries, coarsely chopped

1. Prepare and bake the cake mix batter according to package directions, using a greased 13x9-in. baking pan.
2. In a small bowl, add boiling water to the gelatin; stir 2 minutes to completely dissolve. Cool cake on a wire rack 3-5 minutes. Using a wooden skewer, pierce holes in top of cake to within 1 in. of edges, twisting skewer gently to make slightly larger holes. Gradually pour gelatin over cake, being careful to fill each hole. Cool 15 minutes. Refrigerate, covered, 30 minutes.
3. In a large bowl, beat the cream cheese until fluffy. Fold in whipped topping. Carefully spread over cake. Top with strawberries. Cover and refrigerate for at least 2 hours before serving.

1 PIECE 306 cal., 16g fat (6g sat. fat), 54mg chol., 315mg sod., 37g carb. (22g sugars, 1g fiber), 5g pro.

BANANA SPLIT BROWNIES

How's this for a dessert? All the joy of a banana split without the mess. Everything in this recipe fits into one pan of delectable brownie bars.
—Constance M. Sheckler, Chestertown, MD

PREP: 45 MIN. • **BAKE:** 40 MIN. + COOLING • **MAKES:** 2 DOZEN

- 8 oz. unsweetened chocolate, chopped
- ¾ cup butter, cubed
- 3 large eggs, room temperature
- 2 cups sugar
- 1 tsp. vanilla extract
- 1 cup plus 2 Tbsp. all-purpose flour
- 1 cup maraschino cherries, chopped

TOPPING

- 1 pkg. (8 oz.) cream cheese, softened
- ½ cup mashed ripe banana (about 1 medium)
- ⅓ cup strawberry preserves
- 1 large egg, room temperature, lightly beaten
- ¼ cup chopped salted peanuts
- Optional: Sliced bananas and additional chopped maraschino cherries

1. Preheat oven to 350°. In a microwave, melt chocolate and butter; stir until smooth.
2. In a large bowl, beat eggs and sugar on high speed 10 minutes. Stir in the vanilla and chocolate mixture. Gradually stir in flour. Fold in cherries. Spread into a greased 13x9-in. baking pan.
3. For topping, in a small bowl, beat cream cheese until smooth. Beat in mashed banana and preserves. Add egg; beat on low speed just until blended. Spread over brownie batter; sprinkle with the peanuts.
4. Bake until topping is set and a toothpick inserted into brownie portion comes out mostly clean, 40-45 minutes. Cool completely on a wire rack.
5. Cut into bars. If desired, serve bars garnished with banana slices and additional cherries. Store in an airtight container in the refrigerator.

1 BROWNIE 262 cal., 16g fat (9g sat. fat), 57mg chol., 101mg sod., 31g carb. (23g sugars, 2g fiber), 4g pro.

LOADED-UP PRETZEL COOKIES

Coconut, M&M's and salty, crunchy pretzels make these loaded cookies unlike any you've ever tasted—or resisted.
—Jackie Ruckwardt, Cottage Grove, OR

PREP: 20 MIN.
BAKE: 15 MIN./BATCH
MAKES: 2 DOZEN

- 1 cup butter, softened
- 1 cup sugar
- 1 cup packed brown sugar
- 2 large eggs, room temperature
- 2 tsp. vanilla extract
- 2½ cups all-purpose flour
- 1 tsp. baking powder
- 1 tsp. baking soda
- 1 tsp. salt
- 2 cups miniature pretzels, broken
- 1½ cups sweetened shredded coconut
- 1½ cups milk chocolate M&M's

1. Preheat oven to 350°. In a large bowl, cream butter and sugars until light and fluffy, 5-7 minutes. Beat in eggs and vanilla. In another bowl, whisk flour, baking powder, baking soda and salt; gradually beat into creamed mixture. Stir in remaining ingredients.
2. Shape ¼ cupfuls of the dough into balls; place 3 in. apart on ungreased baking sheets. Bake 12-14 minutes or until golden brown. Remove cookies from pans to wire racks to cool.

1 COOKIE 295 cal., 13g fat (8g sat. fat), 40mg chol., 311mg sod., 42g carb. (28g sugars, 1g fiber), 3g pro.

MILLION-DOLLAR PIES

This classic pie has become an instant family favorite. I like to replace some of the ingredients with low-sugar versions. Add blueberries for a beautiful Fourth of July pie!
—Laura Wilhelm, West Hollywood, CA

PREP: 20 MIN. + CHILLING
MAKES: 2 PIES (6 SERVINGS EACH)

- 1 can (14 oz.) sweetened condensed milk
- ¼ cup lemon juice
- 1 can (20 oz.) crushed pineapple, well drained
- 1 cup sweetened shredded coconut, toasted and divided
- 1 cup chopped pecans, divided
- 1 carton (8 oz.) frozen whipped topping, thawed (3 cups)
- 2 graham cracker crusts (9 in.)
- Maraschino cherries

In a large bowl, beat milk and lemon juice until blended. Stir in pineapple, ¾ cup coconut and ¾ cup pecans; fold in whipped topping. Pour into the crusts. Cover and refrigerate until set, about 2 hours. Sprinkle with remaining ¼ cup coconut and ¼ cup pecans before serving. Top with additional whipped topping if desired, and garnish with cherries.

1 PIECE 438 cal., 22g fat (9g sat. fat), 11mg chol., 225mg sod., 56g carb. (47g sugars, 2g fiber), 5g pro.

LEMONY LAYER BARS

One of my favorite cakes is a white chocolate cake with coconut lemon filling, dark chocolate frosting and almonds. This version of a seven-layer bar combines all those flavors into an easy-to-eat treat. Using soda cracker crumbs makes the bars a little different. If you prefer a more traditional seven-layer bar, graham cracker crumbs can be used instead of soda cracker crumbs.

—Arlene Erlbach, Morton Grove, IL

PREP: 20 MIN. • **BAKE:** 25 MIN. + COOLING • **MAKES:** 2 DOZEN

- 2 cups crushed unsalted top saltines
- ½ cup butter, melted
- 1 cup white baking chips
- 1 cup sweetened shredded coconut
- 1 cup coarsely chopped almonds
- 1 cup (6 oz.) semisweet chocolate chips
- 1 can (14 oz.) sweetened condensed milk
- ¼ cup lemon curd
- 2 Tbsp. grated lemon zest, divided

1. Preheat the oven to 375°. Line a 13x9-in. baking pan with parchment, letting ends extend up sides. In a large bowl, mix cracker crumbs and butter. Press onto bottom of prepared pan. Sprinkle with the white chips, coconut, almonds and chocolate chips.
2. In a small bowl, combine milk, lemon curd and 1 Tbsp. zest. Pour over chips. Sprinkle with remaining 1 Tbsp. zest. Bake until edges are golden brown, 25-30 minutes. Cool completely in pan on a wire rack. Lifting with parchment, remove from pan. Cut into bars. Store in an airtight container.

1 BAR 245 cal., 14g fat (8g sat. fat), 20mg chol., 98mg sod., 27g carb. (21g sugars, 1g fiber), 4g pro.

PINA COLADA CUPCAKES

These treats are fun and colorful for picnics and potlucks! They can be served as cupcakes or layered into individual dishes to make mini trifles.
—Jennifer Gilbert, Brighton, MI

PREP: 20 MIN. • **BAKE:** 20 MIN. + COOLING • **MAKES:** 2 DOZEN

- 3 large eggs, room temperature, lightly beaten
- ½ cup unsweetened pineapple juice
- ½ cup canola oil
- 1 cup canned coconut milk
- 2 tsp. rum extract
- 3 cups all-purpose flour
- 2 cups sugar
- 2 tsp. baking powder
- ½ tsp. baking soda
- ½ tsp. salt

FROSTING

- 1 cup butter, softened
- 3 Tbsp. canned coconut milk
- 1 tsp. rum extract
- 3½ cups confectioners' sugar
- Optional: Toasted sweetened shredded coconut, maraschino cherries, pineapple wedges

1. Preheat the oven to 350°. Line 24 muffin cups with foil liners. In a large bowl, whisk eggs, juice, oil, milk and extract until well blended. In another bowl, whisk the next 5 ingredients; gradually beat into egg mixture.
2. Fill prepared cups two-thirds full. Bake 18-20 minutes or until a toothpick inserted in center comes out clean. Cool in pans 10 minutes before removing to wire racks to cool completely.
3. In a large bowl, beat butter until creamy. Beat in coconut milk and rum extract. Gradually beat in the confectioners' sugar until smooth. Spread over cupcakes. If desired, garnish with coconut, cherries and pineapple wedges.

1 CUPCAKE 330 cal., 15g fat (7g sat. fat), 44mg chol., 189mg sod., 47g carb. (35g sugars, 0 fiber), 3g pro.

ELEGANT FRESH BERRY TART

This elegant tart was my first original creation. If other fresh fruits are used, adjust simple syrup flavor to match.
—Denise Nakamoto, Elk Grove, CA

PREP: 45 MIN. + CHILLING • **BAKE:** 10 MIN. + COOLING
MAKES: 10 SERVINGS

- ½ cup butter, softened
- ⅓ cup sugar
- ½ tsp. grated orange zest
- ¼ tsp. orange extract
- ⅛ tsp. vanilla extract
- 1 cup all-purpose flour

FILLING

- 1 pkg. (8 oz.) cream cheese, softened
- ¼ cup sugar
- ½ tsp. lemon juice

SYRUP

- 2 Tbsp. water
- 1½ tsp. sugar
- 1½ tsp. red raspberry or strawberry preserves
- ⅛ tsp. lemon juice

TOPPING

- ¾ cup fresh strawberries, sliced
- ½ cup fresh raspberries
- ½ cup fresh blueberries
- 2 medium kiwifruit, peeled and sliced

1. Preheat oven to 375°. Cream butter and sugar until light and fluffy, 5-7 minutes. Add orange zest and extracts; gradually add flour until mixture forms a ball. Press into a greased 9-in. fluted tart pan with a removable bottom. Bake until golden brown, 10-12 minutes. Cool on a wire rack.
2. For filling, beat cream cheese, sugar and lemon juice until smooth; spread over crust. Cover and refrigerate 30 minutes or until set.
3. Meanwhile, for syrup, bring water, sugar, preserves and lemon juice to a boil in a small saucepan. Reduce heat; simmer, uncovered, for 10 minutes. Set aside to cool.
4. Combine the strawberries, raspberries, blueberries and kiwi; toss with syrup to glaze. Arrange fruit as desired over filling. Cover and refrigerate at least 1 hour before serving.

1 PIECE 277 cal., 17g fat (10g sat. fat), 47mg chol., 145mg sod., 29g carb. (17g sugars, 2g fiber), 3g pro.

CHERRY PLUM SLAB PIE WITH WALNUT STREUSEL

I love to make desserts with fruit all summer! If you use store-bought crust, I recommend stacking your two pie crusts on top of each other and then rolling them to the correct size.
—Elisabeth Larsen, Pleasant Grove, UT

PREP: 25 MIN. • **BAKE:** 50 MIN. + COOLING • **MAKES:** 20 SERVINGS

- 1 lb. fresh sweet cherries, pitted
- 4 medium red plums, thinly sliced
- ½ cup sugar
- ¼ cup cornstarch
- 2 Tbsp. lemon juice
- Dough for double-crust pie

TOPPING

- ½ cup old-fashioned oats
- ½ cup chopped walnuts
- ⅓ cup all-purpose flour
- ¼ cup sugar
- ¼ cup packed brown sugar
- 1 tsp. ground cinnamon
- ¼ tsp. salt
- ½ cup cold unsalted butter

1. Preheat oven to 375°. In a large bowl, combine cherries, plums, sugar, cornstarch and lemon juice; toss to coat.
2. On a lightly floured surface, roll dough into a 16x12-in. rectangle; transfer to an ungreased 13x9-in. baking dish. Trim even with rim of dish. Add filling. For topping, in a small bowl, mix oats, walnuts, flour, sugar, brown sugar, cinnamon and salt; cut in butter until crumbly. Sprinkle over filling.
3. Bake 50-55 minutes or until filling is bubbly and crust is golden brown. Cool on a wire rack.

DOUGH FOR DOUBLE-CRUST PIE
Combine 2½ cups all-purpose flour and ½ tsp. salt; cut in 1 cup cold butter until crumbly. Gradually add ⅓-⅔ cup ice water, tossing with a fork until dough holds together when pressed. Divide dough in half. Shape each into a disk; wrap and refrigerate 1 hour.

1 PIECE 279 cal., 16g fat (9g sat. fat), 36mg chol., 155mg sod., 32g carb. (15g sugars, 2g fiber), 3g pro.

STRAWBERRIES & CREAM TORTE

This festive strawberry summer treat is one of my mom's favorites. It wows guests every time, yet is simple to make.
—Cathy Branciaroli, Wilmington, DE

PREP: 25 MIN. • **BAKE:** 15 MIN. + COOLING • **MAKES:** 12 SERVINGS

- ¼ cup butter, softened
- ½ cup plus ½ tsp. sugar, divided
- 2 large eggs, separated, room temperature
- ½ tsp. vanilla extract
- 1 cup all-purpose flour
- 1½ tsp. baking powder
- ¼ tsp. salt
- ½ cup 2% milk

ASSEMBLY

- 2 cups heavy whipping cream
- 1 pint fresh strawberries, hulled and sliced
- ½ tsp. sugar
- Additional fresh strawberries

1. Preheat oven to 350°. Line the bottoms of 2 greased 8-in. round baking pans with parchment; grease paper.
2. In a large bowl, cream butter and ½ cup sugar until light and fluffy, 5-7 minutes. Add egg yolks, beating well. Beat in vanilla.
3. In another bowl, whisk flour, baking powder and salt; add to the creamed mixture alternately with milk, beating well after each addition. Transfer to prepared pans.
4. With clean beaters, beat egg whites on medium speed until foamy. Add remaining ½ tsp. sugar, beating on high until the sugar is dissolved. Continue beating until soft peaks form. Spread over batter in pans.
5. Bake 12-15 minutes or until a toothpick inserted in center comes out clean. Cool completely in pans on wire racks. (Cake layers will be thin.)
6. In a large bowl, beat cream until stiff peaks form. Loosen edges of cakes from pans with a knife. Carefully remove 1 cake to a serving plate, meringue side up.
7. Arrange sliced strawberries over top; sprinkle with sugar. Gently spread with half of the whipped cream. Top with remaining cake layer, meringue side up; spread with remaining whipped cream. Top with whole strawberries. Refrigerate until serving.

1 PIECE 267 cal., 20g fat (12g sat. fat), 100mg chol., 158mg sod., 20g carb. (11g sugars, 1g fiber), 3g pro.

SOGGY SITUATION?

Will the strawberries make the cake soggy? The meringue baked over the tops of the cake layers provide a buffer that prevents the berries' juices from soaking into the cake to make it soggy.

PEANUT PRETZEL TOFFEE BARK

My toffee has been a traditional must-make treat for my family and friends for over 40 years. This was my dad's favorite candy, and I think of him each time I make it.
—Barbara Estabrook, Appleton, WI

PREP: 10 MIN. • **COOK:** 15 MIN. + CHILLING • **MAKES:** 1½ LBS.

- 2 tsp. plus 1 cup butter, divided
- ⅔ cup honey-roasted peanuts, coarsely chopped
- ½ cup miniature pretzels, coarsely chopped
- 1 cup sugar
- 2 Tbsp. water
- 2 Tbsp. honey
- 1 cup 60% cacao bittersweet chocolate baking chips
- Sea salt, optional

1. Line bottom of a greased 9-in. square baking pan with foil; grease foil with 2 tsp. butter. Sprinkle peanuts and pretzels onto foil.
2. In a large heavy saucepan, combine sugar, water, honey and remaining butter; bring to a boil over medium-high heat, stirring constantly. Cook 4 minutes without stirring. Stirring constantly, cook 2-3 minutes longer or until the mixture is caramel-colored (a candy thermometer should read 300° for hard-crack stage). Remove from heat. Immediately pour over peanuts and pretzels.
3. Sprinkle with chocolate chips; let stand until chocolate begins to melt. Spread evenly. If desired, sprinkle with salt. Cool 15 minutes at room temperature. Refrigerate until set, about 30 minutes.
4. Break toffee into pieces. Store between layers of waxed paper in an airtight container.

1 OZ. 169 cal., 12g fat (7g sat. fat), 21mg chol., 92mg sod., 16g carb. (14g sugars, 1g fiber), 1g pro.

p. 121

Bonus: Extra-Big Batch Recipes

RAINBOW GELATIN CUBES

These gelatin cubes are fun to serve and to eat! I vary the colors to match the occasion—pink and blue for a baby shower, school colors for a graduation party, and so on. Kids of all ages snap them up.
—Deanna Pietrowicz, Bridgeport, CT

PREP: 30 MIN. + CHILLING • **MAKES:** 9 DOZEN

- **4 pkg. (3 oz. each) assorted flavored gelatin, divided**
- **6 envelopes unflavored gelatin, divided**
- **5¾ cups boiling water, divided**
- **1 can (14 oz.) sweetened condensed milk**
- **¼ cup cold water**

1. In a small bowl, combine 1 package flavored gelatin and 1 envelope unflavored gelatin. Stir in 1 cup boiling water until dissolved. Pour mixture into a 13x9-in. dish coated with cooking spray; refrigerate until set but not firm, about 20 minutes.
2. In a bowl, combine condensed milk and 1 cup boiling water. In another bowl, sprinkle 2 envelopes unflavored gelatin over cold water; let stand for 1 minute. Stir in ¾ cup boiling water. Add to milk mixture. Spoon 1 cup creamy gelatin mixture over the first flavored gelatin layer. Refrigerate until set but not firm, about 25 minutes.
3. Repeat from the beginning of recipe twice, alternating flavored gelatin with creamy gelatin layers. Refrigerate each layer until set but not firm before spooning next layer on top. Make final flavored gelatin layer; spoon over top. Refrigerate at least 1 hour after completing the last layer before cutting into 1-in. squares.

1 PIECE 25 cal., 0 fat (0 sat. fat), 1mg chol., 13mg sod., 5g carb. (5g sugars, 0 fiber), 1g pro.

PEANUT DROPS FROM THE SLOW COOKER

I got this recipe from a friend. I was surprised to learn these chocolaty candies came from a slow cooker. You'll get dozens of candies from one batch.
—Anita Bell, Hermitage, TN

PREP: 20 MIN.
COOK: 1½ HOURS + STANDING
MAKES: ABOUT 11 DOZEN

- 4 oz. German sweet chocolate, chopped
- 1 pkg. (12 oz.) semisweet chocolate chips
- 4 pkg. (10 to 12 oz. each) white baking chips
- 2 jars (16 oz. each) lightly salted dry roasted peanuts

1. In a 6-qt. slow cooker, layer the ingredients in order listed (do not stir). Cover and cook on low for 1½ hours. Stir to combine. (If the chocolate is not melted, cover and cook 15 minutes longer; stir. Repeat in 15-minute increments until chocolate is melted.)
2. Drop mixture by rounded tablespoonfuls onto waxed paper. Let stand until set. Store in an airtight container at room temperature.

1 PIECE 102 cal., 7g fat (3g sat. fat), 1mg chol., 31mg sod., 8g carb. (7g sugars, 1g fiber), 2g pro.

SAUSAGE CHEESE PUFFS

People are always surprised when I tell them there are only four ingredients in these tasty bite-sized puffs. Cheesy and spicy, the golden morsels are a fun novelty at a breakfast or brunch, and they also make yummy party appetizers.
—Della Moore, Troy, NY

TAKES: 25 MIN.
MAKES: ABOUT 4 DOZEN

- 1 lb. bulk Italian sausage
- 3 cups biscuit/baking mix
- 4 cups shredded cheddar cheese
- ¾ cup water

1. Preheat oven to 400°. In a large skillet, cook and crumble sausage over medium heat until meat is no longer pink, 5-7 minutes; drain.
2. In a large bowl, combine biscuit mix and cheese; stir in sausage. Add water and toss with a fork until moistened. Shape into 1½-in. balls. Place 2 in. apart on ungreased baking sheets.
3. Bake until puffed and golden brown, 12-15 minutes. Cool on wire racks.

1 PUFF 89 cal., 6g fat (3g sat. fat), 14mg chol., 197mg sod., 6g carb. (0 sugars, 0 fiber), 4g pro.

QUICK & EASY

FROZEN CITRUS FRUIT CUPS

Add some sparkle to your next gathering with these sunny citrus treats. The petite cups burst with color and fresh flavor, and they look so cute served in shiny foil containers.
—Sue Ross, Casa Grande, AZ

PREP: 30 MIN. + FREEZING
MAKES: 9½ DOZEN

- 5 pkg. (3 oz. each) lemon gelatin
- 10 cups boiling water
- 5 cans (20 oz. each) unsweetened pineapple tidbits, undrained
- 5 cans (11 oz. each) mandarin oranges, drained
- 5 cans (6 oz. each) frozen orange juice concentrate, partially thawed
- 5 large firm bananas, sliced

1. In a very large bowl, dissolve gelatin in boiling water; cool for 10 minutes. Stir in the remaining ingredients.
2. Spoon into foil cups. Freeze cups until firm. Remove from the freezer 30 minutes before serving.

1 SERVING 48 cal., 0 fat (0 sat. fat), 0 chol., 11mg sod., 12g carb. (11g sugars, 1g fiber), 1g pro.

PEANUT BUTTER OATMEAL-CHIP COOKIES

This cookie is my husband's favorite, my classes' favorite, my colleagues' favorite and, no surprise, my favorite too. The recipe makes a big batch—holiday gifts, here we come.
—Dana Chew, Okemah, OK

PREP: 35 MIN. • **BAKE:** 10 MIN./BATCH • **MAKES:** ABOUT 11 DOZEN

- 2½ cups butter, softened
- ½ cup creamy peanut butter
- 2 cups sugar
- 2 cups packed brown sugar
- 4 large eggs, room temperature
- 2 tsp. vanilla extract
- 6 cups all-purpose flour
- 2 tsp. salt
- 2 tsp. baking soda
- ½ tsp. baking powder
- 2 cups semisweet chocolate chips
- 1⅔ cups (11 oz.) peanut butter and milk chocolate chips
- 1 cup quick-cooking oats

1. Preheat oven to 375°. Cream butter, peanut butter and sugars until light and fluffy, 5-7 minutes. Beat in the eggs and vanilla. In a separate bowl, whisk flour, salt, baking soda and baking powder; gradually beat into the creamed mixture.
2. Stir in chips and oats. Drop by rounded tablespoonfuls 2 in. apart onto ungreased baking sheets. Bake 9-12 minutes or until golden brown. Cool for 2 minutes before removing from pans to wire racks. Store in an airtight container.

1 COOKIE 113 cal., 6g fat (3g sat. fat), 15mg chol., 97mg sod., 15g carb. (9g sugars, 0 fiber), 1g pro.

STORAGE SECRET

The peanut butter in these cookies can affect the flavor and texture of other cookies and treats. That said, consider storing these cookies in their own airtight container.

BIG-BUFFET MEATBALLS

I need only a few ingredients to fix these appetizers. Grape juice and apple jelly are the secret ingredients to jazzing up packaged meatballs.
—Janet Anderson, Carson City, NV

PREP: 10 MIN. • **COOK:** 4 HOURS • **MAKES:** ABOUT 10½ DOZEN

- 1 cup grape juice
- 1 cup apple jelly
- 1 cup ketchup
- 1 can (8 oz.) tomato sauce
- 1 pkg. (64 oz.) frozen fully cooked Italian meatballs
- Minced fresh parsley, optional

1. In a small saucepan, combine juice, jelly, ketchup and tomato sauce. Cook and stir over medium heat until jelly is melted.

2. Place meatballs in a 5-qt. slow cooker. Pour sauce over the top and gently stir to coat. Cover and cook on low 4-5 hours or until heated through. If desired, sprinkle with parsley.

1 MEATBALL 147 cal., 9g fat (4g sat. fat), 20mg chol., 411mg sod., 10g carb. (7g sugars, 1g fiber), 7g pro.

RAISIN BRAN MUFFINS

Who'd believe that muffins this tender and tasty could be quick and easy to make? The cereal adds a touch of sweetness and crunch. These are so nice to have on hand!
—Rosemary McGuire, Anderson, IN

TAKES: 25 MIN.
MAKES: 3½ DOZEN

- 1 pkg. (15 oz.) raisin bran cereal
- 5 cups all-purpose flour
- 3 cups sugar
- 5 tsp. baking soda
- 2 tsp. salt
- 4 large eggs, room temperature, beaten
- 4 cups buttermilk
- 1 cup canola oil

1. Preheat oven to 400°. In a large bowl, combine the raisin bran, flour, sugar, baking soda and salt. In another bowl, combine the eggs, buttermilk and oil. Stir into dry ingredients just until moistened.
2. Fill greased or paper-lined muffin cups two-thirds full. Bake until a toothpick comes out clean, 12-16 minutes. Cool for 5 minutes before removing from pans to wire racks.

1 MUFFIN 204 cal., 6g fat (1g sat. fat), 21mg chol., 355mg sod., 35g carb. (19g sugars, 2g fiber), 4g pro.

MINI SAUSAGE QUICHES

These bite-sized quiches are loaded with sausage and cheese, plus their crescent roll base makes preparation a breeze. Serve the cuties at any brunch or potluck gathering.
—Jan Mead, Milford, CT

PREP: 25 MIN. • **BAKE:** 20 MIN. • **MAKES:** 4 DOZEN

- ½ lb. bulk hot Italian sausage
- 2 Tbsp. minced chives
- 1 tube (8 oz.) refrigerated crescent rolls
- 4 large eggs, lightly beaten
- 2 cups shredded Swiss cheese
- 1 cup 4% cottage cheese
- ⅓ cup grated Parmesan cheese
- 2 Tbsp. dried minced onion
- Paprika

1. In a large skillet, brown sausage over medium heat until meat is no longer pink, 4-5 minutes, breaking sausage into crumbles; drain. Stir in chives.
2. On a lightly floured surface, unroll the crescent dough into a long rectangle; seal seams and perforations. Cut into 48 pieces. Press onto the bottoms and up the sides of greased miniature muffin cups.
3. Fill each with about 2 tsp. of sausage mixture. In a large bowl, combine the eggs, cheeses and dried minced onion. Spoon 2 tsp. over sausage mixture in each cup. Sprinkle with paprika.
4. Bake at 375° for 20-25 minutes or until a knife inserted in the center comes out clean. Cool for 5 minutes before removing from pans to wire racks. If desired, sprinkle with additional minced chives. Serve warm.

1 MINI QUICHE 66 cal., 5g fat (2g sat. fat), 27mg chol., 116mg sod., 2g carb. (1g sugars, 0 fiber), 4g pro.

BAKED BEANS WITH PINEAPPLE

This marvelous recipe is a staple at our neighborhood's annual barbecue.
—J. Hindson, Victoria, BC

PREP: 25 MIN. • **BAKE:** 45 MIN.
MAKES: 30 SERVINGS

- 1 lb. bacon strips, diced
- 1 large onion, chopped
- 3 cans (two 55 oz., one 28 oz.) baked beans
- 2 cans (one 20 oz., one 8 oz.) crushed pineapple, drained
- ½ cup packed brown sugar
- ½ cup ketchup

1. In a large skillet, cook bacon over medium heat until crisp. Remove with a slotted spoon to paper towels. Drain skillet, reserving 2 Tbsp. drippings. Saute onion in drippings until tender.
2. In a very large bowl, combine the beans, pineapple, bacon and onion. Combine brown sugar and ketchup; stir into the bean mixture.
3. Transfer to 2 greased 3-qt. or 13x9-in. baking dishes. Cover and bake at 350° for 20 minutes. Uncover; bake 25-35 minutes longer or until bubbly and beans reach desired thickness.

½ CUP 266 cal., 10g fat (3g sat. fat), 22mg chol., 830mg sod., 37g carb. (18g sugars, 8g fiber), 12g pro.

CROWD-PLEASING BUTTERMILK DOUGHNUTS

Guests will have a touch of nostalgia when they bite into one of these impressive doughnuts. Accents of nutmeg and cinnamon, along with a subtle burst of lemon, make them hard to resist.
—June Jones, Harveyville, KS

PREP: 20 MIN. • **COOK:** 5 MIN./BATCH • **MAKES:** 2½ DOZEN

- 2 cups mashed potatoes (without added milk and butter)
- 2 large eggs, room temperature
- 1¼ cups sugar
- ⅔ cup buttermilk
- ¼ cup butter, melted
- 1 Tbsp. grated lemon zest
- 4 cups all-purpose flour
- 3 tsp. baking powder
- 2 tsp. salt
- 2 tsp. ground nutmeg
- ¼ tsp. baking soda
- Oil for deep-fat frying

TOPPING

- ½ cup sugar
- 1½ tsp. ground cinnamon

1. In a large bowl, beat the potatoes, eggs, sugar, buttermilk, butter and lemon zest until blended. Combine flour, baking powder, salt, nutmeg and baking soda; gradually beat into the potato mixture and mix well.
2. Turn out onto a lightly floured surface; roll out to ½-in. thickness. Cut with a floured 2½-in. doughnut cutter. In a deep cast-iron or electric skillet, heat oil to 375°. Fry doughnuts and doughnut holes, a few at a time, until golden brown on both sides. Drain on paper towels. Combine sugar and cinnamon; roll warm doughnuts in mixture.

NOTE To substitute for each cup of buttermilk, use 1 Tbsp. white vinegar or lemon juice plus enough milk to measure 1 cup. Stir, then let stand 5 minutes. Or use 1 cup plain yogurt or 1¾ tsp. cream of tartar mixed into 1 cup milk.

1 DOUGHNUT WITH 1 DOUGHNUT HOLE 184 cal., 7g fat (2g sat. fat), 18mg chol., 232mg sod., 27g carb. (12g sugars, 1g fiber), 3g pro.

Reader Review

"This recipe is perfect without changing a thing! Absolutely delicious, even the next day,"
—DENISELATHERS, TASTEOFHOME.COM

Index

L

M

N

O

P

Q

R

S

T

V